MW01169033

THE DOUBLE MODEL

Lord, thou hast been our dwelling place in all generations. Before the mountains were brought forth, or ever thou hast formed the earth and the world, EVEN FROM EVERLASTING TO EVERLASTING, thou art God. (Psalm 90:1–2)

How do you go about describing a God that neither has a beginning nor an end?

THE DOUBLE MODEL

A Novel Approach To Godhead

Adimchi Onyenadum, MD

authorHOUSE®

AuthorHouse™ UK
1663 Liberty Drive
Bloomington, IN 47403 USA
www.authorhouse.co.uk
Phone: 0800.197.4150

All scriptures are either from King James Version (KJV), or from the New International Version (NIV), copyright 1984 by International Bible Society.

Published by AuthorHouse 09/01/2017

ISBN: 978-1-5246-6619-4 (sc)
ISBN: 978-1-5246-6620-0 (hc)
ISBN: 978-1-5246-6618-7 (e)

Print information available on the last page.

This work is dedicated to the Dimitris and Nina Alexopoulos family, and to all members of our Suprafamilia fellowship.

The Question

When God was *alone* in eternity, *before* anything known as the beginning came into effect, before it came to His mind to create (thought of creating) anything, how was God? Did He have a Son then with Him?

Godhead

The Seven Divine Dispensations of God

CONTENTS

About the Author

Dr. Adimchi Onyenadum is a physician and a medical oncologist at the University Hospital of Patras, Greece. He was born in Port Harcourt, Nigeria, in 1954. His parents, the late Rev. G. Onyenadum Akwarandu and Mrs. (Rev.) Fidelia U. Akwarandu, were pioneers of the Assemblies of God Church, Nigeria. He attended Evangel High School, Old Umuahia, a boarding school of the Assemblies of God Mission, Nigeria, from where he graduated in 1974 after a four-year schooling interruption due to the 1967 Biafran War. Two years later, he was awarded a government scholarship to study in Europe. He studied medicine at the University of Patras Medical School, Greece, from where he obtained a medical degree in 1986. From there he went on to specialize in internal medicine and later on in medical oncology. After serving as a consultant physician at Patras Municipal General Hospital, he was elected as a registrar in medical oncology at the University Hospital of the University of Patras Medical School. Presently he is a medical director at the Department of Medical Oncology of the same hospital. Dr. Onyenadum is a fervent believer in the Lord and a self-styled Bible scholar as it pertains to the original (Koine) Greek New Testament. He teaches a small home Bible study group. He is a naturalized Greek citizen and has a son who is also a medical doctor.

Acknowledgments

For the past nine years, I have been leading a small home Bible study group called Suprafamilia. The group was started by a Christian sister named Nina Guzman Alexopoulou as a family prayer altar. Together with her husband, Dimitris Alexopoulos, this family prayer grew into a dedicated Bible study group. The family has hosted the fellowship since then at their residence at 9 Alkiviadi Street, Patras, Greece. Brother Dimitris Alexopoulos is a deacon at the Free Evangelical Church of Patras, Greece. The couple, with their three daughters, Mary, Adriana, and Erica, and their grandson, Dimitrakis, have been an immense blessing to me all these years. Apart from being my cherished Christian brethren, they have been a true family to me. This fellowship was instrumental in bringing about the writing of this book.

I want to express my appreciation also of Ms. Mariana Boru of Timisuara, Romania, whose sharpness of mind and dedication to the Lord were very inspiring. The name of our fellowship, Suprafamilia, was derived from her Romanian native tongue.

Finally, I want to express my heartfelt thanks and gratitude to my sister in the Lord Ms. Brigitta Flace Karachristou. Acting as an informal secretary, she painstakingly typed into an electronic form the initial handwritten manuscript of this book. At times she would type for many hours into the night or early morning hours. This not only made it possible then for me to post it, chapter by chapter, sequentially on the Bible Facebook group, but it is the same document you are now reading. I thank her from the bottom of my heart and pray that she may find grace and mercy from the Lord wherever she is.

Preface

Statement of Faith

I am a born-again, full-gospel believer. By this I mean I am a repentant sinner, baptized in water by full immersion in Jesus's name and baptized in the Holy Spirit as first evidenced by speaking in tongues. I also believe I have a couple of spiritual gifts, as the Spirit imparts unto believers. I believe in spiritual gifts like prophecies, visions, dreams, revelations, etc. By grouping I consider myself a Pentecostal/Charismatic Oneness believer. I don't believe in the Trinity, and I will explain why in this book

My Eschatology

I believe in a literal heaven and hell (lake of fire). I am a futurist believer of Revelation. I believe nothing in the book of Revelation has yet been fulfilled. I believe that when Revelation starts as outlined in the seven seals, it will be recognizable. I believe the book of Revelation was written in a perfectly systematic and orderly form and that the events written therein are both allegorical and also literal. I believe in a physical, literal rapture of the Church—the bride of Christ—in the middle of the Great Tribulation. After this, Christ will literally establish His kingdom here on earth and reign for one thousand years—the Millennium. I am a mid-tribulation-rapture, millennial Christian. After the Millennium, God will destroy this earth as we know it and usher in the new heaven and the new earth in which righteousness reigns (1 Peter 3:13) and where the redeemed will live with Him eternally.

The Bible

I believe the Bible is the complete, inerrant word of God to humankind. I believe there are no new truths, revelations, knowledge, etc., outside the written word. Anything that contradicts the Bible must be rejected as false. I believe that new truths outside the Bible can be accepted if they complement the Bible or can be inferred from it. Everything I believe must agree either with the letter of the word or with the spirit of the word. Every other thing, I reject as falsehood. By "every other thing" I don't mean things and concepts that the ancient people were unaware of, like contemporary medical science, mathematics, physics, anthropology, etc. I mean spiritual things bordering on theology, faith, beliefs, ethics and moralism.

The Godhead

I never got up one morning and decided I was going to write a book on the Godhead. It just happened by chance. The year was 2010, and I was a member of a Facebook group called "The Bible." This group had more than 1.5 million members worldwide before their discussion board was discontinued for reasons I never learned. Naturally when the discussion section was stopped, I, and I suppose many others, left the group.

As anybody could guess, Godhead and the Trinity were the hottest and most controversial topics on the discussion board. I was actively involved in most of the debates. During one those "epic wars," I discovered that most people (particularly Trinitarians) didn't know what Trinity was all about. So I started a thread with the following question as the opening post (OP):

> When God was *alone* in eternity, *before* anything known as *the beginning* came into effect, before it came to His mind to create (thought of creating) anything, how was God? Did He have a Son then with Him?

I posted this question at about 2:00 a.m. my local time and went to bed after a few comments. By the time I woke up the following morning, there had been about five hundred comments! The thread lasted about three months and logged in more than five thousand comments!

After painstakingly reading through all of the comments that morning, I started posting my answers. My first three posts constitute the first three chapters of this book. As I was getting ready to write my fourth post, God suddenly placed in my heart to write a book on His nature. He immediately gave me an outline of the book and asked me to turn my three previous posts into chapters and the one I was going to write then would be the fourth chapter. From then on, each subsequent post would constitute a chapter until I had finished the book. All these will be apparent as one reads this book.

I initially called the book a "Facebook book" because I wasn't sure what I was going to write. But by the time I was done with it three months later, I knew I had a name for it: *The Double Model: A Novel Approach to Godhead*. This is the book you are about to read. Nothing of this kind, to the best of my knowledge, has ever been taught by anyone (person, saint, church father, church, creed, group, etc.) from the birth of the church till today. I never heard it from anybody or read it anywhere. It is something unique and novel, a smart theoretical, theological model developed exclusively by me, and I believe it was inspired by God. But it is in the Bible, and I dare to say that nobody can overturn it with scriptures.

Just a few more things about this book:

1. Since it was originally meant to be posts in a public forum, the first chapters may be a bit simplistic and informal.
2. It is made up of seven parts and seventeen short chapters. The average number of pages in each chapter is three, and many chapters are only one to two pages long, so it should be easy to read through the roughly one hundred-page, sparsely written book in two or three days.

3. I discussed Godhead in seven broad divine dispensations[1] that I have captioned as parts (Parts I–VII). Each divine dispensation contains a number of chapters of the book. I didn't invent this division. God revealed to me these dispensations and also provided me their contents. God was different in every dispensation, and His name also changed accordingly! He showed me He was a combination of all theological theories about Him, whether Trinity, Oneness, Jehovah's Witness's theology, Binitarianism, Unitarianism, Universalism, etc. It depended on under which of His seven divine dispensations one was examining Him.
4. One may rightly wonder why I consider myself a Oneness believer if I believe God is a bit of everything. Yes, I am Oneness, but not the traditional Oneness, which I believe is false. (It denies the existence of the Father and the Holy Spirit.) My brand of Oneness is highly scriptural and is based on the irrefutable biblical axiom,

---

[1] By dispensation I mean a specific period of time in which God reveals himself in a specific way. Human dispensations are such revelations as they pertain to man and his relationship to God. God revealed Himself gradually and progressively to man from the "fall" till the present age, and will continue to reveal himself until eternal life comes. God is always "different" in every dispensation. Divine dispensation in this book refers to an attempt to discuss God in ephemeral time frames. Accordingly, divine dispensation would be a specific period of time during which God presents or manifests himself as a specific divine entity. This presentation or manifestation would change from one divine dispensation to another as He unravels his divine plan for all creation.

"The Lord God of Israel is *one God*, and there is none else beside him" (Deut. 6:4, Isa. 45:5, Mark 12:29). This biblical Oneness is the winning theology of the Godhead, and this will be made obvious at the end of this book. So please make sure you read the whole book before you dismiss it as fallacy.

5. Finally, I will repeat here a challenge I put forth several times during the original debate on Facebook. I challenge anyone who finishes reading this book to show me any verse relating to Godhead in the whole Bible, from Genesis to Revelation, that my model cannot explain.

Dr. Adimchi Onyenadum

Patras, Greece

Part 1

The Dispensation of Eternity

Chapter 1

The Father

The beginning of Genesis refers to the creation of the earth. The beginning of John 1:1 is the "beginning" of eternity. But before this beginning, before God ever thought of creating anything, when He was alone in the far eternity, did He have a Son with Him then named Jesus or any other name? For sure, no! God didn't have a Son then. He also didn't have angels with Him then, because angels were also created beings.

The beginning was also a created entity! We should not forget that God existed and still exists in an eternity outside time and space. Time had to be created, and space had to be created. Time had to be created for there to be a beginning of any type. So did God have a Son before the first beginning? The answer is a resounding no! God was alone; He didn't have a Son, but He had His word—His spoken word. People have arbitrarily named this "word" Jesus. This is unscriptural. We all know that the person called Jesus had his beginning at Bethlehem, even though He had all the deity dwelling in Him. The "word" before the beginning was not personified in any way as a being separate from God but was equal to Him in a mysterious way, as the Trinity doctrine teaches. The word was simply the spoken word of God.

God was a living being. He was alone, He had His word, and He had His Spirit. He was made up of His word and His Spirit. Just as our own words are not different individuals from us but are part and parcel of us, so God's word was an integral part of God. God's word was God (John 1:1)!

This is simple and biblical. There are no mysteries, no complications. The great confusion is with Jesus, the Son. Who is He? When did He come into the scene? What is His relationship to His Father? If my answers to these questions are right, then the rest of the story is easy to imagine. The discovery of the true Jesus may shock many Christians. It will definitely be scary to traditional, dogmatic Christian parochialism.

But those who are wise will understand.

—Daniel 12:10

Part 2

The Dispensation of Time-Space

Chapter 2

The Son

The question to be considered is this: who is Jesus, and what relationship does He have to God the Father? Of course, this is the great confusion of Christendom.

Having shown in the previous chapter that the word is not a being but the spoken word of God, I will now show that the word *became* a separate spiritual being that is distinct from God the Father.

As God, who was made up of His word (spoken word) and His Spirit, was alone in His eternity (no time, no space), He sort of woke up one day and thought it would be good to *create something.* Only with the thought of it, creation became a reality in the mind of God. That marked the first beginning. *Time* and *the first beginning* were created at that point. Together with the time and the first beginning, and probably preceding them by "split seconds," the Word Being was created.

The first creature God brought into existence was His own word or part of His word (spoken word). He turned a portion of His spoken word into a separate spiritual being from Himself. He gave birth to Him. So the spoken word of eternity then became the Word Being called the Son of God. He was called the Son of God because He came out of God. ("I came forth from the father" [John 16:28].) He was born of God. He was the beginning of every beginning. But He Himself also had a beginning, because He didn't always exist as a Word Being but as the spoken word. I don't believe there is any other way to explain Colossians 1:15, which says, "Who is the image of the invisible God, the *firstborn* of every creature." And Revelation 3:14 (KJV) says, "These things say Amen ... the *beginning* of the *creation* of God."

Having been created (as the Jehovah's Witnesses teach) or born (as the Trinitarians believe) through Him, God created every other thing that was created. You could actually call Him a co-creator since the Bible calls Him and His father creators (Gen. 1:1; Col. 1:16).

Note! Nowhere does the Bible say that the word or the Word Being was named Jesus Christ. But the Word Being was known as the Son of God even before He came in flesh.

> You are my son; today I have become your father.
>
> —Psalm 2:7

> Who hath ascended up into heaven or descended? Who hath gathered the wind in his fists? Who hath bound the waters in a garment? Who hath established all the ends of the earth? What is his name and what is his son's name, if thou canst tell?
>
> —Proverbs 30:4

After His creation, the Son, together with the Father, then created every other thing. I suppose they started from angels, the universe, principalities, powers, and finally earth and man. This explains the plural of Genesis 1:26: "And God said, Let us make man in our image, after our likeness." Perhaps it also explains all the other divine plurals of the Bible (Gen. 11:7, Isa. 6:8, etc). Because from the time the Son was born, He has remained a separate entity from His Father till now, and He will remain so until He finishes the work for which He was brought into being. And then what happens can be anybody's guess.

Chapter 3

The Holy Spirit

Now we are going to examine the third person of the Trinitarian Trinity: the Holy Spirit. Between the three components of the Godhead, the easiest to comprehend and the least misunderstood is the Holy Spirit. The original three hypostases of God (by hypostases I mean essences) are God the Father, His word (spoken word), and His (Holy) Spirit. (The latter two are Gods inasmuch as they are an integral part of God.)

So the above, with its three dimensions, is the one true and eternal God. He was singular—an integer God united in Himself (Oneness Christians believe this) and alone in eternity. We have defined the Father (corresponding roughly to the body). We have defined the word (corresponding to soul). Now we can define the Holy Spirit (corresponding to spirit).

The Spirit is a force (as the Jehovah's Witnesses and others believe) or power that issues or emanates from the Father. It is the life force of God. It is the essence of God. It is invisible. It doesn't have a form or shape.

In contrast, God the Father, even though He is also spirit, is a spiritual being and has form and shape. The Greek word for spirit is *pneuma,* meaning "air" or "breeze."[2] That is the Holy Spirit. Of course, in spiritual and metaphysical terms, "spirit" has acquired a number of meanings like mind, consciousness, the Supreme Being, and that non-quantifiable substance or energy present individually in all living things.[3]

From the three things that make up God, the Father is the only being; the other two are components. He is a spiritual being; He is a living being. He has an essence (substance). He has a form, a shape, and a body (all spiritual). He has qualities and characteristics of a living being. (That is why we are also living beings, because we were made in His image and likeness.) He could talk, think, see, feel, act, etc. He is a living being made up of a spiritual body (1 Corinthians 15:44 says, "There is a natural body, and there is a spiritual body"), His word and His Spirit. So the first divine entity is God the Father.

We have established above that the Holy Spirit is an active invisible force or pneuma that proceeds from the Father (John 15:26). The spoken word resembles the spirit. Just like our own words are invisible, so is God's spoken word invisible, without a substance. Words can be heard, but you can neither see them

---

[2] Silvia Benso, "The Breathing of the Air: Presocratic Echoes in Levinas," in Levinas and the Ancients (Indiana University Press, 2008), p. 13.-14.

[3] Wikipedia.org/wiki/Pneuma.

nor feel them. The difference is that the spoken word of God was made a Word Being. That is, it was made substantive. It was personified. The word was made a separate being beside the Father. He was born and christened "the Son of God" or "God the Son" (as the Trinitarians would have Him). We are yet to see Him undergo other (further) transformations. That is why He is called the "stone of stumbling and a rock of offense, even to them which stumble at the word" (1 Peter 2:7 KJV).

Whereas the Father is a being and the Son is a being, the Holy Spirit has always remained a force and the active power of God. Even though there are physical manifestations of it in several scriptures (see John 1:32–34 and Acts 2:3 for examples), it was never personified in the same way the word was. But as an integral part of the Godhead, it was and is true God (Acts 5:3–4). So the term "God the Spirit" that Trinity believers use is acceptable and biblical.

To recap, when God was alone in eternity, before it came to His mind to create anything whatsoever, He was a unity and didn't have a Son named Jesus with Him. He was, however, a living being (body, form) and could talk (spoken word). He also had a spirit (Holy Spirit) that made Him a living being! When God decided to create, the first thing He created was the Word Being. That is He turned His word (or more correctly, part of His word) into a separate being. This

Word Being was known as the Son of God. The Holy Spirit remained what the name implies: the active power or Spirit of God. It was never personified. So at the creation of man, there were God the Father and God the Son (two separate beings). Of course, the Holy Spirit was there as an inseparable part of God that issues from Him and fills the whole universe.

Chapter 4

Before Genesis 1:1

Till now we have examined three chapters on the Godhead as follows. Chapter 1 dealt with God the Father before eternity began. Chapter 2 introduced the Word Being or the Son of God. His creation marked the beginning of time and space, and of all creation. Finally in chapter 3, the person and nature of the Holy Spirit were defined and examined briefly.

Before I take up Genesis 1:1, which is the only beginning we know well and my next topic, I would like us to examine briefly a time period starting from the time the Word Being (Son) came into existence to the creation of the earth (Genesis 1:1). This time period I have tentatively named the dispensation of time/space. What and how was Godhead during this period? How was the Son, and what was His role?

There are indications from the Bible that before God created anything, He first of all had the following thought: *I will create heaven and earth, angels, principalities, powers, etc. I will create man in My image and for My glory. I will put him in charge of the earth. He will sin, and he will die. I will reproduce myself by making my word a separate being from me. At the appropriate time, this Word Being will be made flesh and born like all other mortal beings. He will do the perfect sacrifice that I require to save man etc.* The rest of the story is well known to a certain extent. The rest of this book will attempt to unfold this grandiose divine plan right into the farthest eternity.

As had been stated already, once God thought it, the Son became a reality, a second spiritual being alongside God. As also has been stated, God is a spirit Being; that means he has a form and shape. The same is true of the Word Being and of angels. They have a form and shape like God, and hence they are called "sons of God" (Job 1:6; 38:7).

An important question here is: what is the form of God?

It couldn't have been anything different or glaringly different from our own form and shape! I am sure many will disagree with this idea. But has anyone ever wondered why God insists on resurrecting our bodies? After all, souls and spirits are alive in heaven without their natural bodies. God wants to redeem our bodies because they are part of Him. Has anybody ever imagined what the human body (with hands, feet, eyes, etc.) was before it was given to man, when God alone possessed it? It is mind-boggling!

So the son of God existed with His Father in a spiritual bodily form that was at that point *unique* only to the Father (He—the Son—was the second being to acquire that body). Then the angels followed, at least some, with the same spiritual body (1 Cor. 15:39–44).

Even though the Son was equal to the Father as the spoken word of God, as the Word Being, however, He was lower than the Father (but higher than the angels) because he was begotten of the Father. The relationship between a father and his son is always that of someone higher to his subordinate. It is never that of equality. The father is always senior to his son *at all times*! So it is with the Godhead, unless there are other laws governing the fatherhood of the Godhead that are unknown to us. But I don't think there is any other law because the concept and model of parenthood was given to us by God, who was the first parent! If you are a father, you require respect from your son (Mal. 1:6). That is hardly any relationship of equality!

Existing by God's side as a distinct being, the Son would look exactly like or somehow like the angels He created. He mixed with them and did errands of His Father with them, just like every child would do with his household, even though he was the inheritor of His father's throne. We infer all these from His appearances in the Old Testament, as we will examine later. He was just like an heir who is a child. The Bible says, "He is no different from a slave, although he owns the whole estate. He is subject to guardians and trustees till the time set by his father" (Gal. 4:1–2 NIV). Good examples are English princes who, in order to sit on the English throne as youths, have to serve in the military with the common people, etc. In the same way, the Son, even though true God and an heir of God's vast kingdom, had to do chores with the angels (Daniel 7:13–14, 10:4–6) until the appointed time.

So was the Word Being an angel? Was He Archangel Michael, as the Jehovah's Witnesses (JW) say? Of course he is not. The Bible states expressly in Hebrews 1 that the Son was superior to angels (v.4).

> For to which of the angels did God ever say, "You are my son; today I have become your father." (v. 5)

> Again when God brings his firstborn into the world, he says, "Let all angels worship him." (v. 6 NIV)

Of course only God is to be worshiped. Angels cannot be worshiped. Angel cannot worship angel (Revelation 22:8-9). So the word was not Archangel Michael. However, the truth is that before coming into the world as a human being, as a spiritual being, He looked very much like the angels. He shared the same body and form with them. At times he was indistinguishable from them. (Compare Rev. 1:13–16 with Dan. 10.) No wonder then the JWs call him Archangel Michael, even though Gabriel would have been more appropriate (Dan. 8:15-16; 9:21; 12:7). They believe he is both the son of God and the angel of God, Michael. This unfortunately is one of those inconsistencies that have characterized Christian Christology from time immemorial. The theology of Trinity also abounds with such antitheses.

Conclusion

The Son existed in a body shape form near His father. This body resembled that of the angels, with whom He interacted freely. He probably led them in various chores and errands for His father, as a prince who was getting ready to be an heir.

This situation continued until He and His father created the earth and man. During this period, the Holy Spirit never changed form or function.

Part 3

The Dispensation of Creation

Chapter 5

Genesis 1:1

In the last chapter (chapter 4) I wrote in my introduction the following:

Before I take up Genesis 1:1, which is the only beginning we know well, and my next topic, I would like us to examine briefly a time period starting from the time the Word Being (Son) came into existence to the creation of the earth (Genesis 1:1). This time period I will tentatively call the dispensation of time/ space. What and how was Godhead during this period? How was the Son, and what was His role?

In this chapter we are going to examine that point in time when God actually created the earth and put humans in charge of it. We should not forget that before now, the creation of the earth and man was only existent in the mind of God. Meanwhile He had created all other things created. Man was the last. So we are now going to examine the Godhead in the dispensation of creation.

Genesis 1:1 opens with the words: "In the beginning God created the heavens and the earth."

The "heavens" could probably refer to our atmospheric space. Since God probably had already created the heavens (which He and His angels inhabited) and the stars and galaxies before He created the earth, the "light" and "stars" and "sun" and "moon" of Genesis 1:14 would probably be referring to making the heavenly bodies visible from the earth, or exposing the earth to them. It could safely be assumed that when "God created the heaven and the earth, the earth was without form and void" and was covered in a cocoon of cloud and darkness, totally invisible to the rest of the universe.[4] The creation of "lights in the firmament" on the fourth day of creation would then be like an unveiling ceremony of a new product.

This "beginning" of Genesis 1:1 is our own beginning. But it is not the beginning of God's creation, as we have already seen. So when God (Elohim) said, "Let us make man in our own image, in our likeness" (Gen. 1:26), He was referring to Himself and to the Word Being, the Son, whom we have already shown was a distinct being from His Father.

The phrase "in our image" shows that the speaker, God the Father, had someone else with Him who was an

---

[4] The Septuagint, the Greek translation of the Hebrew Old Testament, seems to make this claim. It renders Genesis 1:1 in the following way: "In the beginning, God created the heavens and the earth. The earth was invisible and unformed" (Septuagint O').

exact image of Himself—and guess who that person was? I will allow the Bible to answer the question: "He is the *image* of the invisible God!" (Col. 1:15). Hebrews will add, "And the exact representation of his being" (Hebrews 1:3 NIV).

Introducing the "Double"

This is from where I coined the term "Word Being" or "God Being." The one is the Being; the other is the image or the exact representation of the Being! God the Father fully reproduced himself in the Son before the world was made.

This reproduction was important because God was invisible and will always remain invisible to mortals (2 Tim. 6:16). Therefore, it was necessary to create a "second" God! This second God, even though He would have all the qualities of the true God as the word, would be at the same time accessible to man. God duplicated Himself. He made a look-alike or a Double of Himself! The above goes to confirm my assertion that God had a form (body) that was reproduced in the Son and was now to be reproduced in man when God said, "Let us create him *in our own image*." In Genesis 1:26, God created something that looked like Him. The image of ourselves that we see in a mirror is not different from us. The same I suppose applies to God. If what He created had hands and legs and eyes, etc., then it follows that God had the same. Simple logic. And we really see him in various visions in the

Bible having eyes, hands, hair, etc. (Dan. 7:9, Rev. 5:1). So the word *Elohim* in the Old Testament (OT) refers to the Father and the Son. It could have the same or other connotations when used in reference to other deities. We should also not forget that the Holy Spirit was never personified in the Bible, so He was not represented in the "let us" or "in our image" of Genesis 1:26–27 because He simply was not a being distinct from the Father but the dwelling essence of both the Father and the Son.

The above explains the very few places in scripture where God spoke in plural form. (See Gen. 1:26; 3:22; 11:7, Isa. 6:8, Hos. 12:4.) It is noteworthy that three of these cases were in the early part of Genesis (i.e., in the beginning). The last two are in the later part of the OT and deserve some explanation. Hosea 12:4 reads, "He found him in Bethel, and there he spake with US" (KJV). This is probably a wrong translation because both the NIV and the Septuagint have "him" instead of "us." Isaiah 6:8 in the KJV reads, "Also I heard the voice of the Lord, saying, Whom shall I send, and who will go for us? Then I said, here am I, send me." Even though the NIV confirms this reading, the Septuagint does not. It reads, "And I heard the voice of the Lord, saying, Whom shall I send, and *who will go to this people?* And I said, here am I, send me." So in the beginning the Father and the Son were always together and represented together. Gradually, the Father withdrew and left the Son—His double—vested with all His power, name, attributes, etc., to do the rest of the work in the OT.

The Yahweh of the OT is in fact the *Son* (as the Oneness believers believe)! He was a spiritual being—the Word Being, throughout the OT, acting on behalf of His invisible father, and doing errands for Him (doing His will) together with the angels. By the way, this was one of the reasons He was created—to do His father's will, and to represent Him in His dealings with human beings (Heb. 10:9). If God the Father withdrew after Genesis 11:7, then who were the three men of Genesis 18 who visited Abraham? This is a classical argument of Trinitarians in trying to prove Trinity. They say the three visitors represented the Father, the Son, and the Holy Spirit. We have already shown that the Holy Spirit was invisible, was never personified, and can never be represented bodily as a man. There are a few exceptions in which something signified the Holy Spirit (Matt. 3:16; Acts 2:3-4), but we will examine this at a later time. So who were the three men? Let the Bible once again answer the question. One of them was the Lord (Yahweh), the visible form of God (i.e., the Son) (Gen. 18:13, 17, 22, etc.). The other two men (v. 22) were what the Bible said they were—*angels* (19:1)! No difficulties, no mysteries, no Trinity!

From Genesis 11 onward, wherever we see the word *God* or *Lord* (Yahweh), we can use the words *Son* or *Jesus* as a substitute, and we are okay. Because I know many will be quick to disagree, I will give a quick proof of this fact from Hebrews 11:26. It reads, "He (Moses) regarded disgrace for the sake of *Christ* as of greater value than the treasures of Egypt" (NIV).

Which Christ? Was there any Christ in the OT? Yes, He was the perfect substitute! I will treat this topic in detail later on.

To the best of my knowledge, there is no other portion of the OT where God ever again spoke in plural form except in Genesis. If anyone has any such a verse, I will be glad to check it out.

Chapter 6

The Double Model

If we understood how God was in the two previous dispensations—the dispensation of eternity and the dispensation of time/space—then it would be easy to understand Godhead in the dispensation of creation, which we are presently considering. This is a continuation of the previous chapter (chapter 5).

I will now try to show that the Word Being or the Son was a double, a duplicate, or a lookalike of the father—Yahweh. There were two Yahwehs in the Old Testament (OT)—the Father and the Son. Gradually the Father Yahweh withdrew from the scene and left the Son Yahweh to continue His manifestations in the OT

I showed in chapter 5 that the three visitors of Abraham were Yahweh the Son and two angels (Gen. 18:17; 19:1). Then the Lord stood to negotiate with Abraham while the two angels went on to destroy Sodom and Gomorrah. The Bible tells us that as Lot escaped to the land of Zoar, "The Lord rained down burning sulphur on Sodom and Gomorrah from the Lord (father) out of heaven." One Yahweh rained burning Sulphur from heaven from the other Yahweh! Two Yahwehs, one the Father in heaven and the other the Son on earth! It is either we accept this strange but amazing truth of the Bible or we'll have to contend continually with the schizophrenic Christology of the "Jesus-only" group that invented a Jesus praying to Himself.

Because the OT is very vast, I will examine in a random manner various passages that prove that the Yahweh of the OT was in reality the Word Being or God the Son.

In Isaiah's vision of the Lord in Isaiah 6, he clearly saw Yahweh seated on a throne and the seraphs calling out one to another: "Holy, Holy, Holy is the Lord Almighty" (v. 3). The apostle John, however, reveals to us that it was not Yahweh the Father that he saw then but Yahweh the Son, who at the time of John's writing was already incarnated as Jesus Christ (John 12:39–41). Another example is Malachi 3:1. It reads:

> "See, I will send my messenger who will prepare the way before me. Then suddenly the Lord you are seeking will come to his temple; the messenger of the covenant, whom you desire, will come" says the Lord Sabaoth. (NIV)

Who was speaking here? The Lord Almighty. Who appeared in the temple in fulfillment of this prophecy? The boy Jesus. In Luke 2, the boy Jesus suddenly appeared in the temple at the age of twelve and asked his parents:

> "Didn't you know I had to be in my father's house?" But they did not understand what He was saying to them. (vv. 49–50 NIV)

Of course they didn't understand (just as many through the centuries didn't, and still don't understand) because apparently, they hadn't read Malachi! And as it stands, many still have not read Malachi! But Jesus for sure knew, because He knew the scriptures from infancy, just like Timothy (2 Timothy 3:15).

There is therefore no doubt that there are two distinct beings in the Bible called God (some Christians don't believe this, but that is another topic). But we also know that God is one (Deuteronomy 6:4, Mark 12:29). So if this second God is God, then He must be the true God. The only theology that vouches for the above without violating the axiomatic principle of one God is my proffered model. This model states that God duplicated Himself, or gave birth to a second God.

> No-one has ever seen God, *the only begotten God* who is at the Father's side has made him known. (John 1:18, *The Greek New Testament*, Kurt Aland, fourth revised edition)

This second God was an exact image of God the Father (Col. 1:15, Heb. 1:3), a mirror image of Himself, if one prefers this expression. So both father and son are God, and living beings - the father-God and His mirror image, the son-God. And Zechariah declares, "In that day shall there be one Lord, and His name one" (Zech. 14:9 KJV).

This gives the impression that until "that day," there will be more than one Lord (!) and His names many (Rev. 3:12; 19:12, 16)!

My treatise thus far is, to the best of my knowledge, the only working model that can explain almost anything in the Bible concerning the Godhead. It uses Binitarianism to combine Oneness and Trinity into one glorious Unity.

Part 4

The Dispensation of the Church

Chapter 7

The Man—Jesus

In the previous chapter, we determined that God the Father had given birth to His Son in eternity before the world was created. In Genesis 1:1 He created our earth. In Genesis 1:26, He and His Son, the Word Being, created man in their image and likeness. After the first part of Genesis, God the Father gradually withdrew from the earthly scene, bequeathing all His authority to His Son, including His name, Yahweh (Heb. 1:4).

We have also shown, I believe, beyond every reasonable doubt that the Yahweh of the OT is the Word Being or God the Son. So till now, we have seen God when He was alone in eternity without a son or without anything created. Also we have examined the birth of the Word Being (the Son) that marked the beginning of the dispensation of time/space. Next, we saw Godhead at creation. This dispensation of creation spanned Genesis 1:1 till the close of the OT in Malachi.

In this chapter we are going to examine only briefly again the nature of Godhead in the New Testament (NT), a period I will call the church dispensation or the dispensation of grace, as is more commonly known theologically. This period, for the purposes of this book, starts in the gospel of Matthew and ends at the rapture of the church. We belong to this dispensation.

How was, and is, the Godhead during this period?

Jesus was the Yahweh of the OT whom Malachi prophesied would suddenly come into His temple (Mal. 3:1). So the Almighty Yahweh of the OT became the baby Jesus born in a manger in Bethlehem, or the boy Jesus from Nazareth. How could this be? Nobody knows! This was the great mystery of godliness: "God was manifest in the flesh" (1 Tim. 3:16). There is no other mystery about Godhead except this. This mystery was never revealed to the apostles and has never been revealed to anyone else since then. The puzzle, I suppose, will be solved in heaven. The only thing we know is that God prepared for Himself a human body and got in (Heb. 10:5)! We have already shown that the Father had "retired" to heaven, leaving the stage wholly to the Son in His dealings with men. Now in the NT, the Word Being or the Son "was made flesh and dwelt among us" (1 John 1:14).

The big question then is: Who was this Jesus of Nazareth? Was He a man? Was He a god? Was He both?

That He was a man, nobody has ever doubted that. Even the unbelievers and atheists believe that Jesus was a historical figure that was born two thousand years ago and lived and died. Of course they don't believe in the virgin birth and resurrection. So concerning the humanity of Jesus, there is 100 percent agreement on all sides. The big argument is on whether He was God or a god at the same time.

Christians make a lot of fuss when "infidels" dispute the divinity of Jesus, and they are right to do so. What they fail, however, to realize is that Jesus Himself and the Bible as a whole were very particular about emphasizing His humanity rather than His divinity. This was not because His divinity was less important but because that alone wouldn't have been enough to secure our salvation. Did God not create Satan? He did. Would it have been a big deal for Him if He also defeated Satan? Of course not. So what would have been special about Jesus-God defeating Satan? Nothing special. But if a human being, the man-Jesus, with a natural body that was corrupted with sin, a seed of the woman-Eve, could defeat the devil, then that would be the greatest feat of all times. And that was exactly what Jesus did. So we can see why it was more important for Jesus to stress more His humanity than His divinity. How many Christians know this? How many Christians understand that Jesus was wearing the same flesh we are wearing (Rom. 8:3; Heb. 2:16–17, 4:15)? This is a knowledge that changes theology! It is knowledge that will change our relationship with our Savior. It is knowledge with a tremendous transforming power in the life of every believer.

Now that we have ascertained that He was a real man, let us examine whether He was at the same time God.

That Jesus was God is a fact of the scriptures. Those who want to doubt this can go ahead and doubt it. We have already shown from Malachi that the boy in the temple was the Yahweh of Malachi. Also the angel's message to Mary and His miraculous conception (Luke 1:31) testify to His divinity, to mention only these two supporting facts. The bone of contention is the relationship between His humanity and His divinity.

The term *God-man* has been used for centuries to describe Jesus, even though it is not a biblical term. It belies a frantic effort by theologians to explain the seemingly irrational symbiosis between God and man in the same individual. The word itself supposes, or at least implies, the occurrence or existence of the two natures (God-nature and man-nature) in Christ. Thus it is assumed that both natures are intertwined in Christ. The modus operandi of such a strange union as the term *God-man* implies must be inseparability of the two components, something like a mosaic! Nothing could be farther from the truth. Jesus was not a God-man in this sense. He was not a mosaic, and He couldn't be for obvious reasons. He was rather 100 percent man and 100 percent God. He had two parallel natures within Him. His manhood He inherited from His mortal mother, Mary, while His divinity came from His immortal Father, God. The two natures were parallel and independent. They didn't mix. They could communicate, and He could use either at will. They were nonetheless independent of each other. They were both at His disposal during His earthly life, and He could choose which of the two to use at a given time and situation.

The question is with which of His two natures did He live His life on earth? The answer is: with His human nature *only*. While many may disagree with this statement, the truth is that this is the answer. I challenge anybody reading this book and who disagrees to come forward with anything that Christ did here on earth that other human beings cannot do. The only things He did on here on earth that proved He was God were the things He said and of course His resurrection from the dead, never again to die (Romans 1:4). Only His words revealed His divine nature. He lived like a man but spoke like a god! Only a god could have said the things Jesus said. He was either a god to say the things he said (and the way He said them), or He was a downright *lunatic*! Of course we all accept He wasn't a lunatic, so we conclude He was a god; and if a god, then He was the *one and only God*, because God is *one*!

Chapter 8

The Proof of a Lone God

In further analyzing the church dispensation, it is important to briefly consider once more the various dispensations of Godhead as has been developed in this book till now.

In the dispensation of far eternity, the Godhead consisted of God *alone*. We have argued in favor of the fact that He didn't have a Son then. If we can prove this beyond any possible doubt, then the mystery of the Godhead would have been solved beyond any reasonable doubt. And that is what I am going to try to do in this chapter.

The Bible says that in the beginning God had the word with Him (John 1:1). Trinitarians say this word was a being named Jesus. But there is no biblical support for this claim, so it must be rejected as unbiblical. Then we have to accept that this word was His spoken word since we know that God speaks (Isa. 45:23). He was *one*, He was *alone*, and He *spoke*. The spoken word of God was an inseparable part of God just as my spoken word is part of me. We can't see words, we can't touch them, but we can hear them and feel their effects. The same is true of the Spirit of God. It, as well as the word, when considered in isolation, are "things," forces, invisible qualities of God, that are, however, inseparable and substantial components of God. They, and many other qualities of God, are vital to the very existence of God. They make up God! Without them there will be no God! That is why each and every one of them, taken in association with God, is every inch God in itself. So wherever you have God, you can substitute "the Word" or "the Spirit." The difference between the word and the spirit is that the spoken word at a point in time became a separate being from God. He became the Word Being or the begotten Son. The Spirit, on the other hand, has always remained a force (power) that issues from God the Father and the God the Son (John 15:26). The Holy Spirit was never personified at any time.

Now let's take another example. In the beginning God also had a name. But I have never heard anybody claiming that the name of God was a separate being from God. The name was better qualified to be a distinct being from God than the word because, unlike the word (which had no name), the "name had a name"—Yahweh (Gen. 6:2–3)! To make the point even more complicated, God Himself sort of personified "the name." Even though we all know that God inhabited the temple of Solomon (Deut. 12:5, 11, 21), the Bible expressly shows that "the heavens, even the highest heavens cannot contain you. How much less this temple I have built" (1 Kings 8:27 NIV). Apart from Solomon (above), the NT also confirmed this fact. Paul wrote:

> The God who made the world and everything in it is the Lord of heaven and earth and does not live in temples built by hands. (Acts 17:24 NIV)

Of course God could not by any means live in a manmade temple. So who was the inhabitant of the temple of Solomon? The Name (see 1 Kings 9:3 NIV below)! The name of God—*Yahweh*!

> I have heard the prayer and plea you have made before me; I have consecrated this temple which you have built, by putting my Name there forever. (1 Kings 9:3 NIV)

In spite of this tantalizing suggestion of distinctness of "the name," no one has come up with a bizarre theology of a distinct being of the Godhead called "God the Name" and separate from the Father. So why all the confusion about the word of God and not about the name of God? Because the name of God, like the Spirit of God, was never at any time personified, in contrast to the word of God, which was transformed into a separate being.

> And the word was made flesh and dwelt among us. (John 1:12)

I want to believe that I have now convinced someone that the word was the spoken word of God. That spoken word sometime in the far past became a Word Being and coexisted with the Father. He was present with Him at creation as His Word Son, a separate spiritual entity. Sometime after creation, the Father withdrew from the scene and left the Word Son spiritual being with all the authority to represent Him in His dealings with human beings. In addition to inheriting *everything* pertaining to the Godhead, He also inherited the eternal name of God, Yahweh.

> Being made so much better than the angels, as he hath by inheritance obtained a more excellent name than they. (Hebrews 1:4 KJV)

His father was Yahweh in heaven while He was Yahweh on earth. This OT Yahweh (the Word Son) was the being turned into a baby boy in the NT. So the Godhead in the NT consists of God the Father in heaven, the Holy Spirit, the essence of God, and the *man* Jesus Christ.

It is important to note that with the conception of Jesus by Mary, the Word Being *ceased to exist*! He was transformed into, or replaced by, the baby boy and later man Jesus. The Yahweh of the OT is now only a historical figure! He has appeared in His temple in a bodily form. "And the Lord whom ye seek, shall suddenly come to his temple" (Mal. 3:1; see also Luke 2:22–23, 46). He would remain so until His resurrection from the dead. All this while, even though the spoken word of God has undergone all these transformations (from spoken word to Word Being, to OT Yahweh, to man), He didn't cease to be the eternal Word of God, the true and *only* God of the Jews and the Christians. Why? Simply because the active force or the essence of the three real transformations of the Word mentioned thus far (i.e., the Word Being, the Son Yahweh, and the man Jesus), is the spoken word of God, without which none of these three *manifestations* of the Godhead would have been possible.

Before I take up my next topic, which will be the name of God in the NT, I want to invite anyone who has a Bible verse he/she feels contradicts my model or is not satisfactorily explained by it to bring it forward, and I will be glad to examine it. I don't want to claim that my theory can explain everything in the Bible, but it should be able to explain almost every scripture that pertains to Godhead.

Chapter 9

The Name of God, Part 1

Does God have a name? If yes, what is God's name?

Does God's name have anything to do with the Godhead?

We will answer these questions and many more in this chapter.

There is only one sect in Christendom that sort of peddles God's name, not necessarily for profit. This is the Jehovah's Witnesses (JW). They insist that God's name is Jehovah, and as such should be used in worship. Their church bears the name. They talk about it, preach it, worship with it, pray to it, etc. They have even translated their own Bible, restoring the name Jehovah instead of the traditional Lord (there are other English translations that have also done the same). Are they right or wrong? We'll see.

On the other side is the rest of the Christian church. Most, if not all, insist that the name of God in the NT is "Lord," or any of the myriads other qualities of God like the "I am," the "Alpha and Omega," our "heavenly Father," the "almighty God," etc. Some, for example, the Pentecostal church I worship in, insist that even the word *Yahweh* was only the Hebrew name of God. According to them, it applied only to the Jews and not to the Christians. They cite the Septuagint as proof; since it didn't have the word *Yahweh* in it, it meant that the name was not meant for Christians to use. Are they right? What does the Bible teach on this issue?

Of course God has a name, and that name is *Yahweh*. He introduced himself as such:

> God also said to Moses, "I am the LORD (YAHWEH). I appeared to Abraham, to Isaac and to Jacob as God Almighty (El-Shaddai), but by my name the LORD (the Yahweh), I did not make myself known to them." (Exodus 6:2 NIV)

The NIV footnote on Ex. 3:15 reads, "The Hebrew for LORD sounds like and may be derived from the Hebrew for 'I am' in verse 14."

Other sources[5] add that the word *Yahweh* or *YHWH* (Tetragrammaton), as it is more properly known, sounds like the third-person singular of the Hebrew verb "to be" or "I am." So "I am" in third person singular form becomes "He is." Accordingly, the name

---

5 • https://en.wikipedia.org/wiki/Tetragrammaton#cite_note-Knight.2C2011-1
• Knight, Douglas A.; Levine, Amy-Jill (2011). The Meaning of the Bible: What the Jewish Scriptures and Christian Old Testament Can Teach Us (1st ed.). New York: HarperOne. 0062098594.

"Yahweh" should translate "He is"; that is, "the One Who Is" or "the Self-Existent One"! God simply *is*! He has no past, and He has no future. *He just exists in an eternal present*! That is what it means to be eternal and infinite. It is therefore no wonder He said Yahweh was His eternal name (Gen. 3:15). Nobody can change it. It cannot change. Changing it will mean changing God, and this cannot happen, "For I am the Lord, I cannot change, therefore ye sons of Jacob are not consumed" (Mal. 3:6 KJV). We should not forget that in the OT, names usually followed their bearers (see Jabez's case in 1 Chronicles 4:9–10 for an example). Anybody ever wondered where the Jews got this tradition from? Well, from God Himself!

God's name was so important to God that the third article of the Jewish Decalogue was dedicated to it (Exodus 20:7). Death penalty accompanied its misuse.

> And the son of an Israelitish woman, whose father was an Egyptian, went out among the children of Israel: and this son of the Israelitish woman and a man of Israel strove together in the camp; And the Israelitish woman's son blasphemed the name of the LORD, and cursed. And they brought him unto Moses: (and his mother's name was Shelomith, the daughter of Dibri, of the tribe of Dan:) And they put him in ward, that the mind of the LORD might be shewed them. And the LORD spake unto Moses, saying, Bring forth him that hath cursed without the camp; and let all that heard him lay their hands upon his head, and

> let all the congregation stone him ... And he that blasphemeth the name of the LORD, he shall surely be put to death, and all the congregation shall certainly stone him: as well the stranger, as he that is born in the land, when he blasphemeth the name of the LORD, shall be put to death. (Leviticus 24:10–16)

Interestingly and amazingly, God was still that particular about His name even in the NT. In the Lord's Prayer, which could rightly be called "Christ's Decalogue," the third article was also dedicated to the name of God (Hallowed be your *name,* Matt. 6:9). So why didn't the name *Yahweh* occur in the NT if it was that important? The full answer is outside the scope of this book. But for the purposes of this study, I will give a brief explanation.

Because of the capital punishment accompanying the misuse of the divine name, the Jews gradually developed a tradition of avoiding pronouncing the name, even when they read their scriptures. Because they could not just jump over the name when they met it in scriptures, they vocally replaced it with the word *Adonai*, meaning Lord. When the generations that introduced this tradition died, the succeeding generations gradually forgot the way the name was pronounced. It is known that ancient Hebrew was a "consonant-only" language. There were no vowel points in written form. Vowels were verbally supplied by the speakers or readers of a text. As stated above, since they avoided pronouncing the word *Yahweh* for the fear of misusing it and consequently incurring the death penalty, whenever they encountered the name during scripture reading, they replaced it with the word *Adonai*, which meant Lord. With time, the correct pronunciation of the divine name was lost. When the OT was to be translated for the first time from Hebrew to Greek in the third century BC (the translation known as the Septuagint), the seventy-two or so translators could not agree on the exact pronunciation of the divine name, the Jewish Tetragrammaton, YHWH. So they followed the oral tradition of the Jewish fathers by translating the name as LORD (Adonai). That was why the Tetragrammaton was not to be found in the Christian Bible, because all the evidence points to the fact that the first Greek-speaking apostolic church used as its sole Bible (before the Pauline epistles were written) the Septuagint. Even though it would seem unlikely that Jesus ever spoke Greek, yet all His references to the OT were relayed to us by the divine writers of the NT in roughly their Septuagint rendering. For this and many other reasons, we are led to conclude that for some dispensational reasons, it was irrelevant to God whether His eternal name was used in the NT or not.

Now that we have understood the history of the absence of the divine name from the Christian scriptures, we can now ask the question: Why? What could be the dispensational rationale for this great omission?

There are three possible answers:

1. God accepted the replacement of His name with the word *Lord*. Accordingly, "Lord" would be the NT's name of God, as the majority of Christians accept and teach.
2. Name was not important to God in the NT. He could be called anything. It didn't matter to Him, as long as we accepted the Lord Jesus as our personal Savior (many Christians believe this).
3. God had a new dispensational name, which He wanted to introduce instead of His eternal name (my premise).

The biblical odds are against the first two possibilities (the explanation of which is once more outside the scope of this book). So the third should be right: God has a new dispensational name. That is the topic we are treating in this chapter.

God Has a New Dispensational Name

What proofs do we have about the above statement?

The disappearance of God's name from the civil and religious life of ancient Israel was manmade. God wanted His people to use His name, worship with it, and reverence it. He didn't say, "Don't use it," but "Use it carefully." Reverence it! But man always knows better than God! He will always go a step further than God. He will either add to or subtract from God's explicit commands. Eve added, "And you must not touch it" (Gen. 3:3), which God never said. In the NT, Jesus condemned the hypocrisy of the Pharisees, who supplanted God's commands with their traditions. God said: "Honor your father and mother." They said, "If you have something to give to your parents but you give it instead to God as a gift, you are okay. You don't need to bother anymore about your parents," "nullifying the word of God for the sake of your tradition" (Matt. 15:4–6 NIV). So it is plain that God cannot accept the nullifying of His word by any human tradition.

The question then is why didn't Jesus correct this very serious mistake? He was certainly aware of the Greek translation of the OT. Probably many learned rabbis and Pharisees of His time knew and probably used this translation during His time. All the Jews of the Diaspora who attended the three Passovers that Jesus celebrated during His earthly life probably quoted from the Septuagint as they worshiped in the temple with Jesus. Certainly that must be the version the Ethiopian eunuch was reading in his chariot when Phillip met him (Acts 8:30–33). The offense of changing the third commandment regarding God's name was so grave that Christ would have certainly called attention to it. The gospel writers would have definitely recorded a Christ's "woe to you Scribes and Pharisees" on it. They didn't. That Jesus didn't condemn it means that it was God who allowed His eternal name to disappear! The only reason He would do that was if He was introducing another name by which He wanted to be known by in the NT. Yes! That was exactly what He was doing. That name was to be *Jesus* (Yeshua)!

Jesus is the name of God in the NT!

The truth of the above statement will be proved in the next chapter.

Chapter 10

The Name of God, Part 2

The previous chapter (chapter 9) opened with two questions:

1. Does God have a name? If yes, what is God's name?
2. Does God's name have anything to do with the Godhead?

A detailed answer was given to the first question.

In this chapter, we are going to examine the second question: *What has God's name to do with Godhead?*

We will also answer an additional question: *What is the connection between the name of God and the Godhead?*

The whole Christian world (with very few exceptions) believes that Jesus is the Son of God (Christianity is based on this fact). But many doubt that He was God and others still that He was the true God.

What we are going to do in this chapter is to prove that the name of God in the NT is "Jesus" and not

"Yahweh." If we can prove that, then we have proved beyond all doubt that Jesus is the Yahweh of the OT and therefore the Almighty God of the universe. (The "Jesus only" [JO] people should be with me on this!)

Christ consistently talked about the name of God, or "my father's name" or "your name." In Acts of the Apostles and in the rest of the NT, the emphasis shifted from God's name to the name of Jesus. Whereas Jesus made a lot of fuss about God's name or His father's name, from the birth of the church at Pentecost till the end of the epistle of Jude, to the best of my knowledge, any reference made to the name of God was either directly quoted from the OT or a direct or indirect reference to it. The only name that was known to the Christian church was the name of Jesus. In Revelation we once more see direct references to God's name. But the book of Revelation belongs to a different dispensation, as we shall see later.

To start with, what does the name "Jesus" mean?

Jesus is the Greek form of the name Joshua or Yeshua. Yeshua is a compound name derived from Yahweh and Hoshea (deliverance). So the name Yeshua (Jesus) means: "The Lord is salvation" or "Yahweh is salvation." The name Jesus can then be translated as "Yahweh who saves." This follows that Jesus is the *form* or *manifestation* of God that saves.

We know from the Bible that God introduced Himself as the Savior of Israel. He didn't say He was going to send to them a savior apart from Himself. "I, even I, am the LORD, apart from me there is no savior" (Isa. 43:11 NIV). (See also verses 3, 14; Hosea 13:4.)

If we accept that it was the Father speaking in the OT, then it is evident He was the one who came as a babe in the NT. If my model is right, and the speaker in Isaiah 43:11 was the Word Son (the Father's double), then it is even more explicit that this Word Son was the one incarnated in the NT. Either way, the biblical axiom of "one God" is not violated. But the Bible tells us nobody has ever seen the Father: "And my father who sent me has himself testified concerning me. You have never heard his voice or seen his form" (John 5:37 NIV).

We therefore conclude that the Yahweh of the OT whom many saw in the OT (see Ex. 24: 9–11; 32:11, 19–23) was in actuality the Word Son, who later became the Yahweh Savior (Jesus). So when we use the word *Jesus*, we are in effect affirming that Yahweh the Almighty God is the Savior. It couldn't be different if God's Word were to stand without a breach. Any other explanatory model of the Godhead will always leave questions unanswered.

Having understood what the name *Jesus* means, it is easy to understand why it was an important name.

First, because it carries the eternal name of God—Yahweh.

Second, it denotes what God was about to do in the new dispensation—salvation of humankind.

Finally, it shows that the person bearing the name is no other than the Almighty God of the OT come in flesh.

For all practical reasons, God wanted to be known by this name in the NT. It is a dispensational name. His eternal name never changed; neither did He cease to be God the Father in heaven. But for the purposes of the universal salvation he was inaugurating, He wanted to be known as *Jesus* (Yahweh the Savior). It was the only name lost sinners like us could relate to. The word *Yahweh* as the Jehovah's Witnesses (JW) use it wouldn't mean anything to many. Maybe it can inspire awe when you learn its etymology, but it would never have the personal flavor the word *Jesus* has. Even if you don't know the etymology of Jesus, just the fact that the person bearing the name died for you says it all! My mother in a village in Africa adored the name more than ninety years ago when she heard what Jesus did for her. At her ninety-three today, she is still "madly in love" with the name. She didn't have anybody in 1929, when she met the Lord, to teach her what the name Jesus meant, and she still doesn't know. But she adores the name and worships it just for the person it represents.[6] That is exactly God's

[6] She passed away on January 2016 at the age of ninety seven.

plan. He said about His firstborn: "Let all the angels worship him" (Heb. 1:6).

The JW have refused to worship the name. They will be surprised in heaven (they say they are not going, but they are going nonetheless!) when they find out that both Yahweh and the Lamb (Jesus) are worshiped together. And that day, they and all other deniers will worship both the name and the person that bears it (Phil.2:10).

There is no doubt that Jesus made every effort to introduce his name as the name of the Father. Of course he needed a lot of care. He would not dare to declare boldly that he was the Son of God, not to talk of being the true God. How would He then say that His name was the name of God? Just calling God His father earned him the death penalty (Matt. 26:63–66); how much more claiming "Jesus" was the name of the God of Israel! That would have been unheard of and would have earned Him instant death by stoning. Stephen's case was a glaring example. He was summarily executed just for declaring that he saw the Son of Man standing on the right hand of God (Acts 7:55–60). That was why Christ spoke in riddles, parables, innuendos, and varied cryptograms. Some of them He interpreted to his disciples (John 16:25, 29); others He left for the Holy Spirit to reveal to the yet-to-be-born church (John 16:12–13; Matt. 28:19–20).

Now let's look at some of the Bible portions that support our argument thus far:

> No one knows the son, except the father, and no one knows the father except the son and those to whom the son chooses to reveal him. (Matthew 11:27)

This is a very strong statement in the Bible.

Jesus is in effect saying here, "Folks, whatever you knew about God till now, forget it. I am the only one in the world who knows Him. Unless I tell you, you wouldn't know a thing about Him."

So didn't Abraham know God? Didn't Moses, David, the prophets know Him? His answer would be *nope*! None of them knew the Father. The person they knew was the Word Being/Word Son or the Father's double (i.e., *Jesus*)! That was why He said, "If you want to know, ask me, and if I choose I will show you. Otherwise … nothing!" When Philip asked in all sincerity, "Lord, show us the Father and that will be enough for us" (John 14:8), what answer did he get? "Don't you know me Philip …? Anyone who has seen me has seen the Father" (v. 9).

In other words, if you've seen Him (Jesus), you've seen Him (the Father). You don't need to know more! To the Pharisees who asked him, "Where is your father?" He replied, "You do not know me or my father. If you knew me you would know my father also" (John 8:19).

I would add, "For no one knows the father except the son and those to whom the son chooses to reveal him" (Matt. 11:27).

In John 14:21, however He declared:

> Whoever has my commands and obeys them, he is the one who loves me. He who loves me will be loved by my father, and I too will love him and show myself to him.

Judas (not Iscariot) was surprised by this announcement. After all, they were with Him and they knew Him well. Well, not really, because He had declared earlier on that nobody really knew Him except the Father. So we need the Father to reveal the real Christ to us and vice versa. Judas then asked, "What do you mean, Lord?" Jesus replied, "If any one loves me, he will obey my teaching. My father will love him, and we will come to him and make our home with him" (vv. 22–23).[7]

We should note the conditions:

1. Love God.
2. Obey His teachings.

Otherwise you will never comprehend the Godhead. It is a question of revelation from God Himself. This is what you are presently reading—*a revelation of the Godhead.*

Thoroughly scriptural, sound doctrine!

---

[7] All scriptures in this chapter are from the NIV.

Chapter 11

The Name of God, Part 3

In chapter 10, we examined in some detail the name of God, the name of Jesus, and Jesus as a person. The detour was necessary because the three are tightly interwoven. We saw that God's name was connected to Jesus's name. Therefore God's name has a lot to do with Godhead.

In this chapter, we are going to show conclusively that God has a new name in the New Testament (NT), and that that name is "Jesus."

We have stated earlier that the name *Jesus* was an inherited name. Just as we all inherit our surnames and at times our first names from our fathers. Jesus also inherited His name from His Father (Heb. 1:4). So if Jesus's name is "Jesus," then the name of God is "Jesus"! QED.[8] I am called Onyenadum because that is my father's name. In the same way, Jesus is called "Jesus" because that is His Father's name! Why is this so hard to comprehend? Maybe because we are not

[8] QED, Latin, *quod erat demonstrandum*, for completely proved.

"loving and obeying" enough to be recipients of the divine revelation alluded to in the previous chapter.

Now let's see another truth. In John 17:6 Jesus prayed, "I have manifested thy name unto the men which thou gavest me." And in verse 26 He continues: "And I have declared unto them thy name and will declare it, that the love wherewith thou hast loved me may be in them and I in them" (KJV). Jesus said that He has revealed God's name to His disciples. What name? Has anybody ever wondered which name He was referring to? That He revealed it means that before Christ came, that name was hidden. Many will be quick to answer: "Lord," "Yahweh," "Father," or whatever. Let us allow Jesus Himself to answer the question.

But before we get His answer, let us examine a few salient points in the scripture quoted above. The verses show that:

1. God continued to have a name in the NT.
2. The name was hidden (not known to anybody except to Christ).
3. That name wasn't "Yahweh," "Lord," etc., because these were *known* names of God.
4. Somewhere in the NT Jesus revealed that name to his disciples, "I have revealed your name to those whom you gave me out of the world" (John 17:6, original Greek).

We need to diligently search the NT, especially the gospels, to discover the name that Jesus revealed as being His father's name in the NT. The uncovering of the name should be the end of "all *contradictory* ideas of what is falsely called knowledge" (1 Tim. 6:20). We should not forget that He was not point blank about it for obvious reasons but hid it in words and sentence enigmas (see John 16:25).

Where in the gospels did Jesus reveal this name? We don't need to go far. In verse 11 of chapter 17 of St. John's gospel, Jesus prayed, "Holy Father, protect them by the power of your name—the name you gave me—so that they may be one as we are one" (NIV, original Greek).

Note: It is not by chance that He called God "Father" (Holy Father), so that nobody will miss the fact that whatever He was going to say next would be referring to His father—God the Father. Then He went on to ask God His Father to protect His disciples. By what means was the Father to do this? "By the power of your name" (i.e. by the power of God the Father's name, which name He—God the Father—had given to Him, Christ). In other words, God had a name (that till then was unknown to us). That name He (God the Father) gave to His Son (He inherited it from Him). Now the Son was asking the Father to protect His disciples in the power of that name. So we simply reason: Does Jesus have a name? Yes. What is His name? Jesus (Christ is not a name but a title meaning "anointed one"). And He tells us that the name He was bearing was His Father's name (v. 11). And who was His Father? The Almighty God. *So the name of God in the New Testament, according to Jesus, is Jesus,* unless He had another hidden name that He revealed to the gospel writers and they failed to record it and communicate it to us!

To the best of my knowledge, there is no such other name, "for there is no other name under heaven given to men" (Acts 4:12). So the name of God in the NT is *Jesus*!

This truth permeates the entire NT, and I dare to say that nobody can overturn it with scriptures!

Chapter 12

Baptism in the Name of Jesus

> Repent and be baptized, every one of you, in the name of Jesus Christ for the forgiveness of your sins. (Acts 2:38 NIV)

The above is a very controversial and divisive verse in the New Testament (NT).

What has baptism in Jesus's name got to do with Godhead? A lot!

In this chapter, we are going to see how the above verse is directly connected to the Godhead, and how it confirms everything I have written thus far. It will also settle, I believe once and for all, the debate about the correct baptismal formula.

For roughly seventeen hundred years, Christians all over the world have performed water baptism by reciting the formula: "In the name of the Father, and of the Son and of the Holy Ghost." In the early twentieth century (if I am not mistaken) a sect—the United Pentecostal Church (the UPC)—sprang up that challenged this practice, showing that it was biblically wrong. Among other things, they introduced baptism in the name of Jesus. Since then there has been an ongoing controversy in Christendom regarding which baptismal formula is the correct one, and regarding the general meaning of baptism, for that matter.

Now let's see where traditional Christianity got its baptismal formula from.

Matthew 28:19 reads,

> "Go ye therefore and teach all nations, baptizing them in the name of the Father and of the Son and of the Holy Ghost" (KJV).

Even though some sectarian circles, including some UPC believers, have argued that Matthew 28:19 is not genuine, there is no doubt that it is. This was a direct command from the Lord Jesus Christ. Accordingly, the Christians of the early third century AD adopted this formula in baptism. These early Christians also invented the theology of the Trinity[9]. Tertullian, a Latin theologian who wrote in the early 3rd century, is credited as being the first to use the Latin words "Trinity", person" and "substance" to explain that the Father, Son, and Holy Spirit are "one in essence—not one in

---

[9] https://en.wikipedia.org/wiki/Trinity#cite_note-greek-lexicon-22

Person"[10]. This tradition stood firm until the early twentieth century, when it was overturned by the UPC. They (the UPC) insisted and still insist that the biblical baptism is that done in the name of Jesus according to Acts 2:38.

Who is right? What is the true biblical formula for baptism? What has the whole thing got to do with Godhead?

We will analyze these questions here.

When I ask Christians why they baptize "in the name of the Father, Son and the Holy Ghost" (Matt. 28:19, formula), they answer that it was Jesus's command. When I counter that the apostles apparently did not follow that command, they reply carelessly that they would rather follow Jesus than the apostles, implying that the apostles were wrong. This reply is not only an affront on the apostles of Christ, but it also borders on blasphemy. How could the apostles be wrong? If Christ gave them a command and they failed to carry it out or did something else, then the Bible can no longer hold. Christianity would be a big lie, and we can all go believe something else. Christianity is built on the fact that the entire Bible is God-inspired. The Bible is not contradictory; it is harmonious, and it is infallible.

---

[10] • Against Praxeas, chapter 3". Ccel.org. 1 June 2005. Retrieved 2 January 2012.
• Against Praxeas, chapter 2 and in other chapters,
• History of the Doctrine of the Trinity.

The more logical ones, in answer to the same question, insist that both formulas are equal and mean the same thing.

Others say that the baptismal formula doesn't really matter. Is it really so?

Before delving further into this topic, I deem it fit to state at this point some axiomatic truths of the Bible.

1. The church was born on the day of Pentecost (Acts 2:1–4, 41).
2. Christ lived in the Old Testament (OT) (Gal. 4:4; Rom. 15:8).
3. The apostles understood little or nothing of all that Jesus told them (John 14:26; 16:12–13; Luke 18:31–34; 24:25).
4. The only apologists of the true Christian faith are the apostles (Eph. 2:20; Gal. 1:8; Jude 3).
5. We follow the examples of the apostles as outlined in the NT, from Acts to Jude (1 Cor. 11:1; 1 Thess. 2:14; 2 Thess. 3:7, 9).
6. We don't know Christ outside what was handed down to us by the apostles, especially the apostle Paul (Col. 2:6; Gal. 1:8; Jude 3).

People who doubt any of the things listed here may not continue reading this book. It may no longer make sense to them.

To the rest, I will continue.

Axiom 3 states that the apostles did not understand the things that Christ told when He was with them here on earth, including Matthew 28:19.

In John 14:25–26 Jesus told His disciples:

> All this I have spoken while still with you, but the Counselor, the Holy Spirit whom the father will send in my name, will teach you all things and will remind you of everything I have said to you. (NIV)

It is clear here that the Holy Spirit (given at Pentecost) was going to be their teacher. He would teach and remind them of the things Christ told them. "Teaching" means they were ignorant and needed to be taught. "Reminding" means they were forgetful and needed to be reminded of things. Even the little they understood would soon have been forgotten, and they would need the Holy Spirit (the "Reminder") to remind them. So without Pentecost, they would neither know a thing nor remember anything.

In John 16:12–14 Jesus continued:

> I have much more to say to you, more than you can now bear. But when he the spirit of truth comes, he will guide you into all truth. He will not speak his own; he will speak only what he hears, and he will tell you what is yet to come. He will bring glory to me by taking from what is mine and making it known to you. (NIV)

Here again Jesus was making it clear that He could not burden the disciples with more doctrines and instructions since they were incapable of hearing them, not to talk of comprehending them. Once more, it was the Holy Spirit (the Spirit of truth who was to come at Pentecost) who was to guide them to all truth. Without the Holy Spirit, they wouldn't have *all* the truth. If such was the case, everything written in the Bible would be half-truth or outright falsehood. Thank God the Spirit came and they got the whole truth. Everything the apostles believed and practiced was truth indeed—the whole truth. The Bible is the absolute truth of the universe!

Let us now look at the case of the apostle Paul. He wasn't with Christ from the beginning. He was an enemy and persecutor of the early church. When, however, God called him, he "was not disobedient unto the heavenly vision" (Acts 26:19).

As he continued in Galatians 1:16–17:

> Immediately I conferred not with flesh and blood. Neither went I up to Jerusalem to them which were apostles before me; but I went to Arabia, and returned again to Damascus. (KJV)

There in Arabia Jesus Christ Himself taught him everything he was to preach and everything he was to teach the Gentile church.

He became the only person who could declare:

> But though we, or an angel from heaven, preach any other gospel unto you, than that which we have preached unto you let him be accursed. (Galatians 1:8 KJV)

From all the above, it is clear that the absolute truth of the NT is all the apostles believed and practiced. This is recorded in the NT, from Acts 2 to the end of Jude. Anything they did was right. Therefore, anything they didn't do or teach should be considered falsehood. Nobody can interpret Jesus better than the apostles. This is the faith that "was once delivered unto the saints" (Jude 3), and there cannot be any example for Christians to follow outside the example of the early church as recorded in the Acts of the Apostles and the epistles. We join others in following the examples of these saints, as we "contend earnestly" and uncompromisingly for this faith (Phil. 3:17; Jude 3).

So whose example are we following, that of Jesus or that of the apostles?

The above is a fake and unrealistic dilemma because there is no dilemma at all. The apostles carried out exactly the commandment of Jesus in Matthew 28:19 concerning baptism. We on our part follow the apostles as they followed Jesus (1 Cor. 11:1; 1 Thess. 2:14).

Here is the explanation. Jesus left no example on this issue for us to follow. He only gave instructions to His apostles, which they carried out as they were taught by the Holy Spirit. Whether they were right or wrong in their interpretation of Jesus is not for us to decide. The mere fact that they baptized in the name of Jesus means we should do the same, whether or not we understand the rationale behind it. Just doing it because the apostles did it makes it right! We don't need to understand it or to be able to explain it. So on this count alone, the UPC is right. The rest of the church is wrong on the baptism formula. Whereas there are at least five examples in the NT where new believers were baptized in the name of the Lord Jesus Christ (Acts 2:38; 8:12, 16; 10:48; 19:5; 22:16; 1 Cor. 1:13), there is no single example where anybody was baptized using the formula of Matthew 28:19.

Let us now examine the commandment of Matthew 28:19. Jesus said, "Baptizing them in the name of the Father and of the Son, and of the Holy Ghost" (KJV).

Note: Baptism had to be done in a "name" (singular), not "names"! Father, Son, and the Holy Ghost are not real names but titles—qualities. But even if they were names, baptism would still have to be done in a single name, which would represent the three. So baptism according to Jesus's instructions was to be done in a name, and this name would be the name of the Father, the name of the Son, and the name of the Holy Ghost. Even though baptism was to be administered in a particular name, Jesus never revealed that name to His disciples. Why?

Because He had told them earlier on, "I have much more to say to you, more than you can bear now" (John 16:12 NIV).

For sure they didn't understand all the things Christ told them shortly before His ascension (including Matthew 28:19). So He didn't bother to reveal to them the name. But even if He did, they wouldn't have understood anyway. He would have needed also to remind them later on the day of Pentecost. So He left the name a mystery, to be revealed by the Holy Spirit. When the day of Pentecost came, the Holy Spirit could have told Peter something like the following: "You remember the commandment of Matthew 28:19? You remember that thing about the name of the Father, Son, and Holy Ghost? Well the name is Jesus. Baptize them all (the three thousand) in the name of Jesus. That is the name of the Father, the Son, and the Holy Spirit!"

The moral lesson from this topic is the following:

1. God has manifested Himself to us in three ways: God the Father, God the Son, and God the Holy Spirit. This represents the entire Godhead, or what the majority calls Trinity.
2. The name that represents these *three manifestations* of Godhead or "Trinity" is Jesus.
3. Wherever you have the fullness of Godhead (Father, Son, and Holy Spirit), one can substitute the word *Jesus*.
4. *Jesus* is the name of God in the New Testament!

Now, whether or not baptism in the name of Jesus according to Acts 2:38 is necessary for salvation and whether all the other baptisms done in the name of the Father, Son, and Holy Ghost are null and void are outside the scope of this book.

Part 5

The Dispensation of the Millennium

Chapter 13

Godhead after the Resurrection of Christ and Beyond

It has been conclusively shown, I believe in the previous chapters, that Godhead in the dispensation of grace was fully expressed in the person of the man—Jesus Christ. Accordingly, the name of God in this dispensation is Jesus, and not Yahweh, or any other descriptive name. This dispensational name of God came into effect from the time the angel Gabriel announced to Mary the conception of Jesus.

> You will be with child and give birth to a son, and you will give him the name Jesus. (Luke 1:31 NIV)

This manifestation of Godhead in the person of Jesus was to continue until the death of Christ. After his resurrection, Jesus the Son of Man became glorified. As the exalted Son of God, He sat down at the right hand of God, from where He mediates for us through the Holy Spirit who lives in us (Rom. 8:11). From this post, He is also continuing the work of salvation of unsaved souls. He will be in this mediating position until He finally finishes the work of salvation. The first part of completing this work will be accomplished at rapture. Then the church will be finally saved (1 Peter 1:9). The second part will last from the rapture to the end of the thousand-year reign of Christ on earth.

Right now in heaven, the Godhead consists of two distinct beings: God the Father sitting on the throne, and God the Son (Jesus the Savior, the glorified Christ, the Lamb) sitting or standing by His side and busy with the work of salvation of humankind. Both are worshiped as God. This is reminiscent of when God the Father gave birth to the Word Being in faraway eternity. They coexisted together as distinct beings, each of which was God in every sense. The Godhead will continue that way until the rapture, when Jesus returns to take the church, His bride.

After the rapture, how will the Godhead be?

Before I answer this question, I consider it necessary to first of all clarify the time period designated in this chapter as the millennial period (the dispensation of thousand-year reign of Christ on earth) or the dispensation of the millennium.

This period starts at the rapture and ends at the final Judgment of the great white throne of Revelation 20:11–15. It is divided into two parts. The first part consists of the post-rapture, pre-millennial period of world's history. The second part is the millennium proper. It is the period of the thousand-year reign of Christ on earth as described in Revelation 20.

So what will the Godhead be like then?

Once the rapture takes place, the church that was born on the day of Pentecost comes to an end. The mystery of God, which is "Christ in us," will be accomplished (Col. 1:27), and grace will cease. This mystery is also known as the "mystery that has been kept hidden for ages and generations" (Col. 1:26; Eph. 3:4–11), or the mystery of the church (Eph. 5:32). There will still be salvation after the rapture but not by grace, but by law and by righteousness that comes from the law. (Gal. 3:12; Matt. 25:31–46). This surely reminds us of something—the Old Testament (OT)! Some of the tenets of the OT will come back in full force (Rev. 13:10, 14:13). The world will relive the OT in two phases: the post-rapture, pre-millennial phase, which will be the worst representation ever of the OT, and the millennial phase, which will be its perfection on earth—the perfection of any world government this present world has ever known or will ever know (Ezekiel 40–48). The government will once more become theocratic as God originally designed it for Israel. It will be an OT-based theocracy, but with a new covenant (Heb. 8:8–12).

The Dispensation of the Millennium

Because the characteristic of our earth from rapture to the inception of the "new heavens and new earth" will be the rule of the OT law, I have grouped both periods (the post-rapture, pre-millennial, and millennial periods) together as the "dispensation of the millennium."

What will the Godhead be like during this time? How will God reveal Himself during the first half and the second half of this period? What will be God's name then?

This dispensation is more complicated than the previous ones, and so will be the answer to the above questions.

Jesus died like a man and resurrected like a man. That was why after His resurrection, He was very careful to prove to His disciples that He was a resurrected man and not a ghost: "They were startled and frightened, thinking they saw a ghost" (Luke 24:37).

To this, the risen Christ replied, "Look at my hands and feet. It is I myself! Touch me and see; a ghost does not have flesh and bones, as you see I have" (v. 39).

Of course we know from the Bible that "flesh and blood cannot inherit the kingdom of God" (1 Cor. 15:50), neither can "flesh and bones". So the "flesh and bones" of Luke 24 couldn't be real but was meant to show the apostles that it was the same body that

Jesus had when he was alive that was now so changed, it could transverse walls! This fact is very crucial. He consistently and repeatedly called Himself the "son of man" during His earthly life (John 1:52, 3:14 etc.). After His resurrection, He was still known as the son of man (Acts 7:56). He even introduced Himself in the end of Revelation as "the Root and the Offspring of David" (Rev. 22:16), thereby stressing, even at the *end* of all things, His human origin. In heaven He is still a resurrected human being—part of us, one of us, even though exceedingly exalted above all of us and above all of everything (Phil. 2:9–11). So the resurrected Christ was a glorified man in heaven. He was and is still God's Son in heaven, sitting or standing at His right hand and interceding for us (Col. 3:1; Heb. 12:2; Acts 7:55–56). In heaven He is the mediator between God and us (1 Tim. 2:4–5). The work of mediation cannot be done by a spirit. It had to be a man to mediate between God and man (Job. 9: 32–35), and that *man* was the risen Christ.

We have already seen that Jesus was the Father's double or "lookalike" (Yahweh on earth) who was made flesh. After He became flesh, the earthly Yahweh ceased to exist. The death of Jesus and His burial brought to an end the Son word incarnate. If He wasn't resurrected, that would have been His end! But God resurrected Him. He didn't abandon Him in the grave, "nor did He let his Holy One see decay" (Acts 2:24–27). With His resurrection, He was brought back to life, to an uninterrupted existence, because His body never tasted corruption (Acts 2:31). He continues His existence in heaven as the glorified Son of God or God the Son, still distinct from His Father. So in heaven right now there are two distinct beings that are worshiped as God—God the Father, who is always sitting on his throne, and His Son Jesus Christ, sitting (Col. 3:1) or standing (Acts 7:56) by His right hand. He is either identified as the Son (Acts 7:56) or as the Lamb (Rev. 5:6). They are both worshiped as God (Phil. 2:10–11; Rev. 5:8–13; 22:3).

The Godhead will continue to be the way I have just presented it until Jesus returns for the church on rapture day. From that day and afterward, the church transfers to heaven. From being a church militant and embattled, it becomes a church triumphant and victorious, materializing the "joyful assembly in heaven" (Heb. 12:22–24).

How will the Godhead be from the rapture onward?

It will be the same as before rapture. We will see God the Father sitting on His throne and our first Big Brother Jesus sitting by His right side, poised to take back the kingdom of earth. He had already made all the preparation before coming for us. We now join him as His glorious church or bride. With Him as leader we wage the final battle of regaining the earth at the battle of Armageddon (Rev. 19:14–18). This battle ends with the defeat of the Antichrist and the imprisonment of Satan. Immediately, the thousand-year reign of Christ on earth is ushered in.

So the Godhead during the first part of the millennial dispensation is not too different from the Godhead during the church dispensation. God the Father is still there unchanged (He has never changed and can never change [James 1:17].) Jesus remains the exalted Son of God He has always been from His resurrection. The difference is that then, He will be united with His church bride (married to her [Rev. 21:9]), and fights together with her to regain control over a rebellious earth that is already reeling under God's judgment.

During the thousand-year reign of Christ on earth described in Revelation 20:4–7, Jesus physically reigns on earth with His saints. God will still be God in heaven then. Jesus will be the "second" God or His representative, as He has always been. But He will then be a King reigning on earth from Jerusalem with all His saints.

Conclusion

At birth Jesus was a suffering Savior, the sin-bearer. At resurrection, He was a glorified man sitting at the right hand of God, mediating for us. At the rapture He is a warrior lamb fighting for his kingdom. During the millennium, He is King, sitting on the throne of his father David, reigning for thousand years on earth.

We saw in an earlier chapter that God the Father was unchangeable, whereas God the Son had a beginning; after undergoing several transformations, He will have an end!

The conclusion of this chapter is a proof of the above statement. We have seen the beginning and various transformations of the Word Being. We are yet to see more, and the end!

Note: All this while, there is no personality independent of the Father or of the Son called the Holy Spirit. Neither the Father nor the Holy Spirit has undergone any change or transformation of any type. Only the Word that was made flesh in Bethlehem is now an exalted Savior in heaven and will soon become a reigning monarch in Jerusalem.[11]

---

11 All Bible verses of this chapter, unless otherwise indicated, are from the NIV.

Chapter 14

The Name of God in the Millennium

We have shown that God's permanent and eternal name is the Tetragrammaton YHWH or YHVH or "Yahweh," as is the more commonly accepted pronunciation. It was by this name that He was known throughout the OT. We also showed that this name was changed to "Jesus" in the NT. *So Jesus is the dispensational name of God in the NT.*

As the dispensation of the church closes and the dispensation of the millennium opens, did God once again change His name? Is there a dispensational name of God in the millennial dispensation?

To answer these questions, let us examine what the Bible reveals on them:

> Him who overcomes, I will make a pillar in the temple of my God. Never again will he leave it. I will write on him the name of my God, and the name of the city of my God, the New Jerusalem, which is coming down out of heaven from my

> God, and I will also write on him my new name. (Revelation 3:12)

From the above it is clear that after the events of Revelation 3, God will still have His unchangeable name, but Jesus will have a new name. This will definitely be his name in the new dispensation (new dispensation, new name!). It could be a new name altogether, or it could be just an *additional* dispensational name.

What could that name be?

As always, Bible interprets Bible, so we have to look in the Word to find clues for the possible name. Revelation 19:11–16 reads:

> I saw heaven standing open and there before me was a white horse, whose rider is called Faithful and True. With justice he judges and makes war. His eyes are like blazing fire, and on his head are many crowns. He has a name written on him that on-one knows but himself. He is dressed in a robe dipped in blood and his name is the Word of God ... On his robe and on his thigh he has this name written: KING OF KINGS AND LORD OF LORDS.

In this scripture we notice that the white horse rider, who is no other than Jesus, has four names. First he was called "Faithful and True." Probably the angel or a voice that introduced him to the scene announced him with that name. Something like: "Behold, there comes the Faithful and True witness!" (See Rev. 3:14.) The three other names were written on him. The first was probably written on one of His many crowns and nobody knew it except Himself. The second was written on his blood-dripped robe and is the "Word of God." The third is the expression "King of Kings and Lord of Lords" written on His thigh.

The three of the four names, even though they are called names, are in actuality not proper names but descriptive titles. The apparently *real* name is the hidden one written on His crown. That is His new name (Rev. 3:12), which should be His dispensational name. So if we can decode or decipher it, then we have discovered God's name in the millennial dispensation! Now nobody should tell me we don't have a right to unlock the secret if we can.

There are two passages in the OT that may be the key to finding this name. They are Jeremiah 23:5–6 and 33:14–16. Both speak of a righteous *branch* whose name will be: "The LORD Our Righteousness."

> "The days are coming," declares the Lord, "when I will raise up to David a righteous Branch, a king who will reign wisely and do what is just and right in the land. In his days Judah will be saved and Israel will live in safety. This is the NAME by which he will be called: 'The Lord Our Righteousness.'" (Jeremiah 23:5–6; 33:15–16)

This Branch has been positively identified as Jesus, and all Christians are in agreement on this. Also all Christians, who believe in a literal kingdom of God on earth, agree that the period referred to here ("The days are coming") is the millennium period. So it follows that the Branch's name as revealed in this verse should logically be the new name of Christ during the millennium. And if this is his new name, then the phrase "Lord Our Righteousness" should be the name of God during the dispensation of the millennium.

"The Lord Our Righteousness" in Hebrew is Yahweh Tsidkenu. This is one of the many compound, descriptive names of God in the OT such as Yahweh Nissi (The Lord Our Banner), Yahweh Rapha (The Lord Our Healer), Yahweh Jireh (The Lord our Provider), etc. There is, however, another name in the Bible that stands for phrase, "The Lord Our Righteousness." It is not a descriptive, compound name; it is a real compound name of God like Yeshua (Yahweh-Savior), Jehoash (Yahweh is Strong), Joel (Yahweh is God), etc. Like these names, it was given to Hebrew children in the OT. The name is "Jehozadak" (NIV). In the KJV it is pronounced "Josedech." In the Septuagint, it is rendered "Yosedek". "And this is the name by which he will be called: Yahweh Yosedek" (Jer. 23:6

Septuagint[12]). The name is encountered a couple of times in the Hebrew scriptures (1 Chron. 6:14–15; Ezra 3:2). Perhaps its most prominent occurrence is in Zechariah 6:11, where it was given as the full name of Joshua the high priest: "Take the silver and gold and make a crown, and set it on the head of the high priest, Joshua son of Jehozadak" (Zechariah 6:11 NIV).

The next verse, verse 12, goes on to make a most amazing declaration: "Here is the man whose name is the Branch and He will branch out from his place and build a temple of the Lord!"

Among other things, he (Joshua son of Jehozadak) "will sit and rule on his throne. And he will be a priest on his throne. And there will be harmony between the two"! (v. 13).

Of course Joshua the son Jehozadak was a priest. He was never a king, and he never ruled Israel or Judah. Also there was never a priest and king in Israel. No priest ever ruled Israel. The two posts were

---

12 The tradition of the Septuagint is to do a loose meaning translation of major Hebrew nouns, including the compound names of God. Examples are two incidents in Numbers and Genesis. In the first instance, Numbers 11:3, "the name of the place was called Taberah" (KJV, NIV). The Septuagint translates the Hebrew word Taberah as "burning". In Genesis 22:14, God's compound name, Jehovah Jireh (KJV), is translated as simply "The Lord saw", or The Lord will provide". So it is surprising and at the same time strange that in the verse quoted above, the Septuagint translators left the word Yosedek (which is a compound name of God meaning "Our Righteousness") untranslated, whereas both the KJV and the NIV translated it! Could there be a divine purpose for that?

incompatible. That was why verse 13 was quick to add that "there will be harmony between the two" offices in spite of their incompatibility. Prophet and priest, yes (Ezekiel, Ezekiel 1:2); prophet and king, yes (David, Acts 2:29–31); priest and king, *never*! *Prophet, Priest, King*, Jesus! Only our Lord and Savior Jesus Christ can hold the last two positions at the same time or combine the three offices; no other person. The Trinitarians can enjoy their "three in one" here! No other place!

One last point: Is it by chance that this mysterious high priest of Zechariah has the name "Yeshua" and the surname "Jehozadak"? He strangely combines the two dispensational names of God, Yeshua and Yosedek, in the dispensation of the church and the dispensation of the millennium respectively. The implications of this chapter, especially in relation to Zechariah 6, are more far-reaching than can be addressed in this book.

In conclusion, Jesus has a new name in the millennial dispensation. That new name is written on his crown in Revelation 19 and is known to none other than to him alone. But we are informed that the name is written on the foreheads of his elect 144,000 in Revelation 7, 9, etc. That name would be His new name, or God's dispensational name in the dispensation of the millennium. He will probably have it alongside with the name *Jesus* because the work of salvation will still go on during the millennial period, until "the new heaven and the new earth" appear. Since this name will be the new name of Jesus during the millennial dispensation, it follows that that will be God's new name in the dispensation of the millennium. That name is Josedech ("The Lord Our Righteousness").

Jehoshua YHWH Jehozadak (Hebrew) or
Jesus Yahweh Josedech (Greek),

interpreted as

YHWH Our Savior (Jehoshua – Jesus), YHWH
Our Righteousness (Jehozadak – Josedech).

This will be the name of Godhead in the millennium:

Jesus Yahweh Josedech

Jesus is the true God!

> And the name of the city from that time on will be: "Yahweh Shammah—the Lord Is There." (Ezekiel 48:35 NIV)[13]

[13] All Bible portions in this chapter are from the NIV version of the Holy Bible.

Part 6

The Dispensation of Eternal Life

Chapter 15

An Eternal Life Fantasy

I have finished the strenuous task of defining Godhead in terms of dispensations and tracing it through the various dispensations so far examined. Now I ask your permission to revel for a while in a hilarious fantasy of the approaching *eternal life*.

The dead in Christ have been resurrected (1 Thess. 4:16).

The church has been raptured to heaven (v.17).

The redeemed dead of the tribulation period (Antichrist period) have been resurrected and have reigned with Christ for a thousand years on earth (Rev. 20:4).

The thousand-year millennial reign has been completed (Rev. 20: 7).

The earth has been destroyed following the battle of Gog and Magog (vv.7–9).

Satan has been finally judged (v. 10).

The judgment of the great white throne has been concluded.

Death, the final enemy, has been defeated and thrown into the lake of fire (vv. 11–15; 1 Cor. 15:26).

The *grand finale* has at last arrived.

At this point, the stage is set; the curtains are drawn for the final act—the beginning of the long-awaited eternal life.

Revelation 21 opens with the words, "Then I saw a new heaven and a new earth, for the first heaven and the first earth had passed away" (Rev. 21:1).

This marks the beginning of the new dispensation: the dispensation of eternal life.

Before I examine Godhead in this dispensation, let me describe a washout period between the end of the millennium and the beginning of the dispensation of eternal life.

All the righteous from the general resurrection of the saints, from the rapture, from the great tribulation, and from the judgement of the great white throne, etc., are now safe in heaven with Christ. Then they all come down together with Him in (Rev. 19:14) to reign with Him on earth (Rev. 20:5) for the thousand-year millennial kingdom.

After the millennium, and before the destruction of the earth by fire (Rev. 20:9–11), where were the saints?

Of course back in heaven. One could argue that God took them directly to the new earth and not back to heaven. It could be so. It is not clear whether the new earth is going to be a completely new, *de novo* creation, or whether it is going to be this same planet, refurbished, as the Jehovah's Witnesses (JW) claim. There are pros and cons to the argument. If it is an entirely new planet, then God took the saints there directly before revealing it in Revelation 21. If it is our same planet changed, then during the period of its renovation, believers went back to heaven temporarily because their eventual abode would be the earth, not heaven! I tend to believe that it will be the same earth that will be completely changed for this permanent residence of the redeemed. There is enough evidence in the Bible to support this conjecture, but it is beyond the scope of this book. Whichever way, however, whether it is a new earth or the old earth refurbished, when it appeared in Revelation 21:1, it had already the saints settled in it. After seeing the new heaven and the new earth, John saw in real time something else that was exceedingly very marvelous: a *real* city descending out of the heaven of the new earth, toward the new earth! The city was exquisitely beautiful, brilliant as a precious jewel, transparent as crystal and radiant with the very glory of God (Rev. 21:10–11). This is the holy city, the New Jerusalem, coming down out of heaven from God (v.10). Then he (John) heard a loud voice from the throne saying, "Now the dwelling of God is with men, and he will live with them" (v. 3).

It is from the above that we conclude that when the new earth was unveiled, it already had inhabitants in it—people! The significance of the above verse is that God Himself will also live permanently with His saints on earth! I wonder why the majority of mainstream Christianity feels belittled when the JWs tell them they are going to live on earth and not in heaven. But God Himself will be living on earth with us! And wherever Jesus is "tis heaven there," as one old hymn goes!

Now to our topical question: *How will the Godhead be in this most glorious dispensation?*

Answer: There will still be God the Father sitting on His throne, and Jesus the Son with His myriads of titles (Christ, Faithful, True, the Word of God, King of Kings and Lord of Lords, I Am, Alpha and Omega, Beginning and the End, the Root, the Offspring of David, the Bright Morning Star, to mention but a few), sharing the throne with Him (Rev. 3:21). Apart from the myriads of His title names, He (Jesus) will still have His two proper names, now combined in one—Jesus Josedech! He and His Father will still be separate, distinct beings and worshiped together as God (Trinity). And actually, from chapter 21 of Revelation and afterward, Jesus is referred to only as the Lamb (vv. 9, 14, 22, 23, 27; 22:1, 3). In three of the instances cited (Rev. 21:22; 22:1, 3), the Lamb is referred to together with the "Lord God Almighty" in a singular form (21:22), and both are seen sitting on the *same* throne (Rev. 22:1, 3). This is complete and absolute identification of the Lamb with the Lord! The most characteristic expression to this effect is that of Revelation 22:3, which reads: "The throne of God *and* of the lamb will be in the city, and his servants will serve *him*."

Note: The "*throne*" (one) of "*God and Lamb*" (plural) will be in the city, and his servants will serve "Him" (singular).

The dispensation of eternal life "ends" in Revelation 22:5 with the following words: "There will be no more night. They will not need the light of a lamp or the light of the sun, for the Lord God will give them light. And they will reign forever and ever."

Note: All this while, we have been dealing with two distinct beings—the Father and the Son. The absence of the Holy Spirit even at this close of time is quite impressive. Anything that is revealed in scripture about eternal life as a real process is condensed in the last two chapters of Revelation, and specifically from 21 to 22:1–6. There is no mention whatsoever, even in passing, of the Holy Spirit. Whatever happened to the third person of the Trinitarian Godhead? Simply, the Holy Spirit of the Trinity is nonexistent! There was never a being, much less a person, distinct from God the Father, called the Holy Spirit. The Holy Spirit is not a distinct person from the Father and the Son. "It" was never personified at any time. "It" is the force of the two divine beings, their power, their *essence*.

Without "it," there will be no God. The Holy Spirit is the true God!

This is thoroughly scriptural, and I dare to say that nobody can overturn it with scriptures![14]

---

[14] All Bible portions in this chapter are from the NIV version of the Holy Bible.

Part 7

The Dispensation of Eternity

Chapter 16

The All Saints Convention

As we saw in the previous chapter, all believers have been successfully resettled in the new earth. God Himself and the Lamb are already dwelling with them on the new earth, permanently. The fusion of the New Jerusalem with the new earth underlines this fact. The devil had been finally done away with (Rev. 20:10), as were death and Hades (v. 14). All workers of iniquity (i.e., "everyone whose name was not found in the book of life") have been cast into the lake of fire (v. 15). The New Jerusalem, now located on the new earth, will be out of bounds to anything filthy:

> Nothing impure will ever enter it, nor will anyone who does what is shameful or deceitful, but only those whose names are written in the Lamb's book of Life. (Revelation 21:27)

The Dispensation of Eternity

> There will be no more night. They will not need the light of a lamp or the light of the sun, for the Lord God will give them light. And they will reign forever and ever. (Revelation 22:5)

The above scripture, which in the previous chapter marked the end of the dispensation of eternal life, also marks the beginning of eternity or the dispensation of eternity.

I know it is an oxymoron to describe infinite things like "eternity" and "eternal life" with words like *beginning*, *middle*, *end*, etc., which are very temporal and finite. But we have no choice if we are to make any sense out of these "eternal things." Even God himself used the analogy of day and night to describe the New Jerusalem (Rev. 21:25) in order to make these supernatural concepts a bit intelligible to us.

What will be the nature of the Godhead in this dispensation?

Before we address this question, let us first of all try to *imagine* what "life" will look like during this dispensation. As in other instances in this book, when the Bible is silent, it is going to be *guesswork* that will be based on revealed truths of the Bible.

So here we go.

We saw at the close of the last chapter that God had already settled the saints on the new earth before it was revealed to John (Rev. 21:1). Unlike what people think, the new earth is a real place. It is a real planet hanging in space just like ours. We are going to be real people there, resurrected spiritual beings with spiritual bodies that are capable of inhabiting a spiritual world. The new earth will have buildings (John 14:2), and there will be no more sea (Rev. 21:1). The New Jerusalem is also a real city, with dimensions (Rev. 21:15–17), with foundations, walls, gates, streets, and a square (Rev. 21:10–21). It even has trees and a river (Rev. 22:1–2)! So the new earth and the New Jerusalem are going to be real worlds akin to the one we are used to here. Only this time it is not going to be of a physical but of a spiritual substance. The Bible informs us that we are going to be living permanently on this new earth the way we live here on this present earth. Eternal life is not going to be a boring or scary situation, in which we are going to be dots in the clouds dangling about all eternity. No, we are going to be organized into societies on the new earth as we are here on earth. We will be grouped into nations (Rev. 21:24), cities, communities. There will be kings, presidents, rulers, governors, ministers, judges and officials, and citizens of nations, great and small (v. 26). The eternal kingdom of God is a sprawling, universal, cosmic empire never ever known to humankind. The absolute despot will be the Lord God Almighty and the Lamb. The capital and the imperial seat of this cosmic empire will be the

New Jerusalem. There will be many similarities and differences with our present world. One difference will be that there will be no sea in this new earth. Another difference will be that there will be no sun or moon (Revelation 21:23). But one of the most glorious differences will be that there will be no more sin, and absolute justice will reign (2 Peter 3:13, original Greek).

Probably the first thing that King Jesus Josedech will do in this new world will be to convene a solemn convention of all saints and the entire host of heaven. In this great feast, rewards and praises will be awarded to all saints, from the least to the greatest, according to their efforts while on earth (1 Cor. 3:8–14; 2 Cor. 5:10; Rev. 11:18; 22:12; Matt. 25:31–46).

To get an idea of what this process might look like, let us imagine a situation where one billion people are to receive prizes in one grand ceremony in a stadium. The ceremony starts with the last and least of the one billion. He is called up on the podium to receive his prize. He did nothing while on earth; he achieved nothing. As a matter of fact, he just managed to say "remember me, Lord," as the thief on the cross, before he died. But in spite of this, God orders an angel to give him a prize or even Christ Himself comes and awards it to him. One could imagine his surprise when he sees Jesus walk up and attaches a dazzling golden pin on his/her lapel just for making it to heaven! This is apart from the indescribable and priceless eternal life he/she was already enjoying. At this, the whole convocation erupts into cheers, thanks, praises, and worship. The angels and the host of heaven fall prostrate and worship. "Holy, Holy, Holy, Lord God Almighty" rings from one end of the universe to another. When one praise song ends, somebody starts another song and everybody joins. It will be something like the old time revival meetings on earth. The twenty-four elders are already up from their thrones, with their crowns cast down at Jesus's feet. They are already lying prostrate on their faces, worshiping. I personally will certainly start a song that day (thank God I know a lot), and I am sure every single saint that moment will also like to start a song of worship and praise to Him that sits in the throne, and to the lamb. This will go on and on. At a point the angels, being God's ministering spirits, will remember their duty and will get up from their prostrate position to continue their duty of maintaining order(!) and running the program. They will try to calm the throng of the redeemed enraptured in their gratitude to God. They could say something like, "Okay, folks, we have to go on to the next person, that is, to the number two person" (always from the rear!). But nobody would seem to listen. Why? Because everybody will be feeling the same unworthiness that poor last folk was feeling! Just as that last fellow with the golden shirt-pin would be wondering what he/she ever did to merit such an honor, so everybody from the greatest to the least will be wondering what we ever did to deserve even being in heaven and in such a convocation, not to talk of getting a reward! Then we see the Lamb standing at His father's side; then we remember what He did for us, and then we can't hold back the tears and the praise. We just can't stop! Then, helplessly, the angels look to God for direction. And God may say, "Well, leave them. What can we do?" Then ... whaaa! Glory! Whistling! Shouting! Praises! Hallelujahs! Thunder! Lightnings! It goes on and on for eternity without end! And you can imagine, we are only witnessing the reward of the last and least of all. There are one billion more to follow! That is eternity! As a stanza in the hymn, "Amazing Grace" goes:

> *When we've been there ten thousand years, Bright shining as the sun. We've no less days to sing God's praise, As when we first began.*

No one should tell me I am stretching things too far. There is no other way to explain passages like Revelation 21:24–27:

> The nations will walk by its light and THE KINGS OF THE EARTH will bring their splendor into it. On no day will its gate ever be shut, for there will be no night there. The GLORY AND HONOR OF NATIONS will be brought into it.

This refers to the New Jerusalem.

There is going to be a permanent and eternal convocation in the New Jerusalem. As the convocation goes on, people will be coming and going as they please. It is just like the church of Pentecost and some Christian churches today that have services every day and all week long. These services go on and on, but people come and go as they choose and are able. We will have a foretaste of this form of worship in the millennium when all the nations of the earth will have to make constant, compulsory pilgrimages to the millennial Jerusalem to worship the Lord. Any nation that refuses to go up (there will be such cases) will be punished immediately with the appropriate punishment. Zechariah informs us that if Egypt refuses to go up to Jerusalem to celebrate the feast of tabernacle, they will have no rain plus other plagues (Zech. 14:16–19). This certainly reminds one of the Old Testament. This is one of the reasons I wrote in my millennial chapter that the regime of the millennium is going to be that of the Old Testament law—immediate judgment for every disobedience.

The dispensation of eternity is now in full progress.

God is still God the Father on His throne. Jesus is still God the Son and the Lamb, sharing the throne with his father. They are both still distinct beings separate from each other. They rule together the new earth and the new universe (new heavens), and they are worshiped together as God. Jesus's name is Jesus Josedech. He may have a new sub-dispensational name then, having a specific relationship to His reigning over the new earth. There is no scriptural basis for this assumption, except for a continual and perhaps multiple fulfillment of Revelation 3:12, "I will also write on him my new name."[15] The Holy Spirit has, all this while, remained an unquantified divine entity, since "it" was never quantified or personified in any way or at any time. He remains the essence of the true and holy Godhead.

Read on—we are nearing the "end"!

[15] All Bible portions in this chapter are from the NIV version of the Holy Bible.

Chapter 17

The End

In chapter 16 we left off at where the last and least of our hypothetical one billion saints was being rewarded. This ceremony lasted a whole eternity. Then the second to the last is rewarded. This also will last an eternity. By the time we come to the first person, the champion, (nobody should tell me there won't be a champion. If there is a last, then there must also be a first) guess how much time has elapsed? One billion eternities! Wow! Did you say astronomical figures? Yes, and much more.

The unit of time measure in the dispensation of eternity will be eternity. Just as our highest unit of distance measurement is the "light year,"[16] in eternity everything will be measured in "eternities"—one, two, three thousand, one billion eternities, trillions of eternities, eternities of eternities, etc. If we mortals have developed and can comprehend the concept

[16] The speed of light is 186,300 miles per second or 300,000 kilometers per second. A light year is the distance that light covers when it travels continuously in a vacuum for one year.

of astronomical figures normally expressed in light years, then we sure can imagine celestial time frames expressed in eternities—or at least the physicists and astrophysicists can.

So I come back to the time when billions of eternities have expired and at last everybody has received their reward. All this while, life has been going on normally in the everlasting bliss of the New Heavens and the New Earth. Perhaps after countless more eternities have passed, then the end will come! The time will come for God to revert back to what He was before it came into His mind to create anything created, when He was *alone* in eternity. We are getting back to our starting point, the arbitrary point (beginning) of a perfect circle. The beginning point of a perfect circle? Impossible, because a perfect circle cannot have a beginning. Therefore, another oxymoron.

As the rhetoric question of this book's front cover states, *how do you go about describing a God that has neither a beginning nor an end?*

Well, that is what we have attempted in this book. God gave me an arbitrary starting point or beginning called the dispensation of eternity. From this point He took me on a glorious journey of His seven divine dispensations which I have covered with you in this book. Now, as with a perfect cycle, we are back to our starting point, the dispensation of eternity.

It is important here to recall the initial question of this book.

Question

> When God was *alone* in eternity, *before* anything known as the beginning came into effect, before it came to His mind to create (thought of creating) anything, how was God? Did he have *a Son then* with Him?

The right answer to the question is that He didn't have a Son, but only His word (His spoken word). This word was then turned into a separate being from His Father to carry out a specific function of saving man who was yet to be created. We have shown through scriptures that the Son had a beginning (He was born, created) and will have an end. Now that every wish of God has been completely accomplished, we are now going to witness "the end" of the Word Being or Jesus or King Jesus Josedech.

All this while in eternity we have witnessed the Father and the Son as separate beings, acting together in unison, sharing the throne together, being worshiped together, etc. We all know that they are one and the same being, yet separate and distinct, something resembling Trinity. But the doctrine of Trinity has already been disproved in heaven because there is no distinct being in heaven called the Holy Spirit. (This will be the first doctrine of the Godhead to be disproved in heaven. We will see further down what happens to the other doctrines of Godhead, and who wins in the end.)

In heaven, we'll be asking each other, "Seen the Holy Spirit anywhere?"

And the answer will be, "Nope! No Holy Spirit anywhere. Only the Father and the Son!"

Everybody would admit then that of all the doctrines of the Godhead we were taught on earth (Trinity, Unitarianism, Binitarianism with its JW's variation, and the Jesus only of the Oneness Pentecostals), the first to crash in heaven would be the Trinity. The Binitarians with their JW's variation would seem to be the ones to be vindicated in heaven. The Godhead will be roughly the way they believed it: God the Father and Jesus the Son, the Holy Spirit an invisible force! But somehow in the mind of all of us will be that unbreakable biblical axiom that states that *God is one*: "Hear o Israel, the Lord our God is *one* Lord" (Mark 12:29).

But here they are two in one. How come? So for the Bible to hold true, since "the Scripture cannot be broken" (John 10:35), some time, some "day" one of the two has to go! And who can that one be except the created one, the Son? The thought of our beloved Jesus disappearing or ceasing to exist could be shocking even in heaven. However, this is what 1 Corinthians 15:28 seems to teach: "When he has done this, then the son himself will be made subject to him who put everything under him, so that God may be all in all" (NIV).

So we'll all be waiting for that moment with mixed feelings. Jesus is our Savior. He is one of us. He is our elder brother. He is the only God we truly knew and could relate to. Even if He was going back to a place of greater honor, we still could not imagine Him disappearing. That would be awful even in heaven. We will miss Him!

Then the day arrives. The second person of the Trinitarian Godhead is going to have His end, in the last and greatest ceremony of all.

On that day Jesus is presented as the guest of honor. He is the focus of all creation. All eyes are on Him. At last the Bible is fulfilled where it says that the whole universe was created by Him and for Him:

> For by him were all things that are in heaven, and that are in earth, visible and invisible, whether they be thrones, or dominions, or principalities, or powers; all things were created by him, and for him. (Colossians 1:16 KJV)

Yes, everything was created by Him and *for Him*. He is the sole heir of the entire universe. As a matter of fact, the totality of these seven divine dispensations discussed thus far has only one aim: to give the Son an inheritance.

> But in these last days he has spoken to us by his Son, whom he appointed heir of all things, and through him he made the universe. (Hebrews 1:2)

An angel reads some relevant portions of scripture to help prepare us for what we are about to witness. Yes, there are scriptures in heaven! He certainly reads from Colossians 1:15: "He (Jesus) is the image of the invisible God, the first born over all creation" (NIV).

Then he reads from Revelation 3:14:

"These things saith the Amen, the faithful and true witness, the beginning of the creation of God" (KJV).

And from Proverbs 8:22–23, 25, and 30 which says:

> The Lord brought me forth as the first of his works, before his deeds of old; I was appointed from eternity, from the beginning, before the world began. Before the mountains were settled in place, before the hills, I was given birth … Then I was a craftsman by his side.

The son is the radiance of God's glory and the exact representation of his being, sustaining all things by his powerful word. (Hebrews 1:3)

> For I came out from God and I have come. (John 8:42, original Greek).

I came out from the father and I came into the world. (John 16:28, original Greek).

And many more ...

Then he closes with 1 Corinthians 15:28:

> When he has done this, then the son himself will be made subject to him who put everything under him, so that God may be all in all. (NIV)

He reads all these verses, and preaches extensively on them. Yes, there is preaching too in heaven! The angels and the elders may also take turns preaching and expatiating on these deep scriptures. These Bible sessions may last eternities (you think a one-hour sermon on earth is too long, eh?), since there is no time in eternity! There will be no boredom because people will be coming and going as they please, until that grand moment arrives when all will be required to be present in that last grand convocation of all:

> But you have come to Mount Zion, to the heavenly Jerusalem, the city of the living God. You have come to thousands upon thousands of angels in joyful assembly, to the church of the firstborn whose names are written in heaven. (Hebrews 12:22–23 NIV)

The conclusion of the sermons would be something like this: "We have now ascertained that King Jesus Josedech was nothing more than only an image (the true image) of His Father."

"When you see your image in the mirror, is that person you?"

"Yes!" everybody will answer.

"Is that image a different person from you?"

"No!" we will all echo.

"While on earth, did you ever have a situation where someone could unite himself completely with his mirror image?"

"No!" again the answer will come.

"Then today you are going to witness such a situation. We are going to witness the life image called King Jesus Josedech reunite with His real object, who is the Father."

Hush, silence, and amazement.

Then we see God the Father standing by the right, and his image, King Jesus Josedech, standing by the left, both facing each other. Then the Son Image starts a slow movement toward the Father Object. This movement will be slow and accompanied by continuous praise and worship and hilarious jubilation. This eternal trip of the image to the object may last countless eternities. After all this is heaven and we are not hurrying to anywhere.

Then at last the image is at a close-up to the object: eye to eye, nose to nose, mouth to mouth. Then everybody holds their breath. The whole universe is at a standstill. The greatest event of all time and of all eternity is about to take place. Jesus is going back to the position of glory He had before the world was made: "Father, glorify me in your presence with the glory I had with you before the world was made" (John 17:5).

This is the glory of the spoken word of God. From the preceding preaching, everybody must have understood that John 1:1 referred to this spoken word, but nobody was sure how the whole thing was going to work out practically. If what I am writing here is correct, then probably only those who read and accepted what I have written in our age will know what to expect, because God has revealed it!

> No eye has seen, no ear has heard, no mind has conceived what God has prepared for those who love him—*but God has revealed it to us by his Spirit.* (1 Corinthians 2:9–10)

> For we have not received the spirit of the world but the spirit who is from God, *that we may understand what God has freely given us.* (v. 12)

So nobody should tell me I have no right to write these details since nobody can know them. The above scriptures make it clear that the unregenerated may not know, "but God has revealed it to us by his spirit."

Back to our narration. There is a deathly silence in the entire universe, a split second before the absolute union of the image with the object. At that moment of the union, a thick cloud envelopes the scene.

Then bright, crystal, and dazzling light, and … behold!

There is only one being sitting on the throne, *alone*!

Wow!

Guess who that being is? We won't believe our eyes. Unbelievable!

Jesus!

Then the whole throng of believers, all the heavenly hosts, and all creation erupt into a unified, rapturous, and everlasting worship that will never end.[17]

The "Jesus only" people are the winners!

Jesus is the one true and only God.

The End

[17] All scriptures in this chapter, unless otherwise indicated, are from the NIV.

Glossary[18]

Trinity The doctrine of Trinity teaches that God is one but that He is made up of three divine persons, the Father, the Son and the Holy Spirit[19]. These three are co-equal, co eternal and consubstantial. Even though they are distinct persons from each other, they are nonetheless one. The Trinitarians call this a mystery. Nobody has ever come up with a satisfactory explanation of the mechanism of this mystery.

Binitarianism is a Christian theology that considers Godhead to be made up of two persons. In contrast to Trinity that teaches that there are three persons in one God, Binitarianism posits that there are two persons (the Father and the Son) in one divine substance of God. Classically it is understood as a form of monotheism.

Oneness (Modalism) denies the existence of three persons. It teaches that God is one, who has manifested Himself in three ways, the Father, the Son and the Holy Spirit. There is however only one person, and that person is not the Father but Jesus. Jesus is the Father, the Son and the Holy Spirit. Hence the "nick name": Jesus Only.

---

[18] These are simple, working definitions of the four main theories of Godhead. There are many other major and minor variations of these doctrines, and overlaps are common. The version of Godhead expounded in this book is a variation (my variation) of Binitarianism.

[19] Apart from Trinity, none of the other theories of Godhead considers the Holy Spirit a person distinct from God.

Unitarianism, as the name implies, asserts that God is one (a unity) and there is no other God beside him. Roughly, they understand God the way the Jews understand Him. They reject the deity of Jesus. For them Jesus was a human being inspired by God in his teachings. They accept him as the messiah and the savior of the world.

Printed in the United States
by Bookmasters

Printed in the United States
By Bookmasters